CW01467515

Shining Lights

Student's Book 3

B1+

Emma Heyderman   Niamh Humphreys

Oracy	Challenge	Life competencies	STEAM
Giving encouragement Giving yourself thinking time Organising your answer	We can't always find the right clothes for every situation.	**Digital literacy:** using tools and creating digital content **Creative thinking:** generating multiple ideas **Learning to learn:** using feedback to improve learning	
▶ **Giving a presentation** Speaking clearly and at an appropriate speed Using humour Making positive comments and asking sensible questions		**Creative thinking:** considering multiple perspectives **Learning to learn:** evaluating learning and progress	**Science and Engineering** Does skateboarding defy the laws of physics?
Asking questions Using a range of vocabulary Giving positive feedback	Young people have lost touch with nature.	**Creative thinking:** experimenting with and refining ideas **Critical thinking:** drawing appropriate conclusions	**Science** How do animals adapt to their environment?
▶ **Having a debate** Using confident body language Managing speaking time Identifying weaker arguments		**Learning to learn:** using effective strategies for learning and retaining information **Critical thinking:** evaluating options and recommendations to come to a decision	
Getting everyone's opinions Giving positive feedback Offering examples	Travel is exciting but can be very bad for our planet.	**Critical thinking:** identifying and understanding problems **Critical thinking:** drawing appropriate conclusions	
			Science and Maths
▶ **Giving a talk** Sequencing ideas for structure Using appropriate gestures and body language Engaging the audience		**Creative thinking:** Imagining alternatives and possibilities **Collaboration:** actively contributing to a task	
Using evidence Summarising Listening actively	Some students feel that school is boring and irrelevant for their future.	**Emotional development:** showing empathy for the feelings of others **Critical thinking:** identifying, gathering and organising relevant information **Creative thinking:** elaborating on and combining ideas	
▶ **Participating actively in discussions** Getting everyone's opinion Taking turns Interrupting politely		**Creative thinking:** participating in a range of creative activities **Learning to learn:** using effective strategies for comprehension and production tasks	**Science** What is extreme weather?
Showing interest Justifying your ideas Ending a presentation	Jobs are changing and young people need new skills for their working life.	**Critical thinking:** evaluating options and recommendations to come to a decision **Critical thinking:** participating in a range of creative activities	
▶ **Interviewing** Listening actively Asking open questions Asking follow-up questions		**Creative thinking:** Imagining alternatives and possibilities **Critical thinking:** drawing appropriate conclusions	
			Arts
Digital classroom: Practice Extra			

WELCOME TO SHINING LIGHTS

Learn about the features in your new Student's Book.

VIDEO
Watch interesting videos that bring language to life

LEARNING AIMS
See what you will learn in this unit

ORACY
Learn the skills to become proficient when you communicate

TALKING POINTS
Say what you think about the topics in the unit and listen to others' views

CHALLENGE
Think about, research and resolve challenging issues

CHALLENGE: STAGE 1
Start thinking about the issue you will discuss throughout the unit, ending in a presentation of your findings and discussions

VIDEO
Watch interesting documentaries about a variety of topics

THINK OUTSIDE THE BOX
Read or listen to a text with unexpected ideas and think about it in an original and creative way

HOW IS UNIT 2 SO FAR?
Think about and reflect on what you've learned up until now

DIGITAL ACTIVITIES
Go online to learn and practise more grammar

GRAMMAR VIDEO
Watch grammar videos to practise and improve your grammar

GRAMMAR BOX
Simple grammar explanations

STRETCH
Go a bit further – stretch yourself with one of these fun activities – or all three!

ORACY
Improve and practise your skills to speak in public

LIFE COMPETENCIES
Improve your learning following these useful exercises

EXAM TIP
Read through exam tips to improve your performance

EXAM TASK
Exam task and practice

SELF-ASSESSMENT
Reflect on how confident you are with what you've learned at the end of the unit

IMPROVE YOUR WRITING
Improve your writing following these simple steps

ORACY
Combine and practise all of the oracy skills you've learned in this unit

ORACY VIDEO
Watch real students practising their oracy skills and discussing how well they've done

VOCABULARY REFERENCE
An easy record of all of the vocabulary in the unit

WRAP UP
Take a look back over the unit and reflect on your learning

SUSTAINABILITY
Reflect on what you've learned about sustainability in this unit

LIFE COMPETENCIES
Improve your learning following these useful exercises

CHALLENGE: STAGE 2
Start preparing the issue you will discuss throughout the unit, get into groups and start researching!

CHALLENGE: STAGE 3
Develop your ideas further and prepare a first draft

STEAM INVESTIGATIONS
Learn more about STEAM (Science, Technology, Engineering, Arts and Maths) and investigate different issues

CHALLENGE: STAGE 4
Present your work to the class

GRAMMAR REFERENCE AND PRACTICE
See all of the grammar explained and practise it!

UNIT 1 THE RIGHT FIT

LEARNING AIMS

- **Skills:** discuss and create texts about clothes
- **Grammar:** review present simple and present continuous; state verbs and adjectives: word order
- **Vocabulary:** learn and practise words to describe clothes
- **Creative thinking:** design a website for creating, selling or swapping clothes
- **Exam practice:** Reading Part 2, Speaking Part 2, Listening Part 1

THE CHALLENGE

We can't always find the right clothes for every situation.

You will:

- **Stage 1 Think:** find out about situations where special clothes are important.
- **Stage 2 Prepare:** find different kinds of websites that offer clothes.
- **Stage 3 Develop:** create a website which lets people design, make, sell or swap clothes.
- **Stage 4 Present:** present your website to the class.

1 Look at the photo. Discuss the questions in small groups.

1. Where are the people?
2. Why do you think they are dressed the way they are?
3. How important is it to wear the kinds of clothes you want to wear?

2 Watch the video and find one example of the following:

1. clothes that show support for a team
2. a style that shows how young people are different
3. clothes that show respect for a tradition

▶ 01

CHALLENGE ①-②-③-④

Think

Discuss the questions with a partner and make notes.

1. When do young people want to wear special clothes? Make a list of situations.
2. When is it difficult to get exactly the right clothes?
3. List all the ways you know of finding clothes.

Documentary ▶   **Grammar** ▶   **Grammar** ▶

VOCABULARY

CLOTHES

1 🖥️ 🔊 **1.1 Go to the digital activity and match the words to the photos. Listen, check and repeat.**

buttons   costume   jersey   laces   material
pattern   sleeves   sweatshirt   tracksuit   zip

▶ Vocabulary reference page 16

2 **Two friends are going to a carnival. Complete the conversation with the words from Exercise 1.**

Oscar: Look, I've put on my ¹ _____ for the carnival! I'm dressing up as a clown. I'm not sure about it. I'm afraid I'll be too hot because the ² _____ is really heavy. And the ³ _____ are too long. Maybe I don't need to do up the big red ⁴ _____. And I should wear a T-shirt because this ⁵ _____ under the jacket is too much.

Leo: You look great. I love the colourful ⁶ _____ on the hat. Now look at what I'm wearing.

Oscar: But you're just wearing a ⁷ _____! Are you going out for a run?

Leo: Oh, sorry, I've done up the ⁸ _____, but look, under the jacket, you can see my football ⁹ _____. And I've got a scarf in our town's colours, too! I'm going to the carnival dressed up as our team's biggest fan!

Oscar: But you *are* our team's biggest fan! You look good, but tie your ¹⁰ _____ or you'll step on them and fall over!

3 **Think back to the video. Discuss the questions in pairs.**

1 Which different types of clothes do you see in the video?
2 Whose clothes do you like the best?

4 **Read the conversation and match the verbs in bold to the definitions (A–C).**

Owen: Oh, I like that sweatshirt. It **suits** you!

Andy: Yes, but it doesn't **fit** me. Look, the sleeves are too short.

Owen: Oh, yes. That's a pity because the colour **matches** your new trousers.

A be the right size for somebody
B look good or right on somebody
C be the same colour or type

5 **Complete the text with the correct form of** *suit, fit* **or** *match*.

My sister has finished studying and I'm going to her graduation ceremony. It's formal and I want to wear a dress with a jacket or a scarf that ¹ _____ it. I want a green dress because people say green really ² _____ me. And my favourite shoes don't ³ _____ me anymore, so I have to buy a new pair.

6 **Graduation ceremonies are usually formal. What other formal events do you go to? What do you wear? Tell a partner.**

▶▶▶ STRETCH! **Open your wardrobe. Can you name everything in English? Look up the words if you cannot. Bring your list to the next class.**

7 🛡️ **Digital Literacy** **Find out about the clothes that people wear to celebrate a life event, for example, a wedding, a graduation, etc., in a country that is not your own. What words will you use to start a search? Compare ideas with a partner.**

🛡️ CHALLENGE ①②③④

Prepare

1 Form groups of three to four students.
2 You are going to create a website which offers clothes. Decide what kind of clothes you would like to offer.
3 Agree on what kind of website you will create. For example, it could be a site for selling, borrowing, renting or swapping clothes, or where people can offer their own designs.
4 Go online and find similar kinds of websites. Make notes about the ones you like the best.

READING

SHORT TEXTS

1 Read the description of Jordan. What does he want to buy for his cousin? Which two things does he need to consider before buying a present?

1 Jordan's cousin is leaving for university. He'd like to get her some jewellery but can't afford to spend very much on her. He knows she prefers silver to gold.

2 Read the information about market stalls A and B. Which stall would be the most suitable for Jordan? Why is the other one unsuitable?

☑ **EXAM TASK** READING PART 2

3 The people below all want to buy a present in the market. Read the descriptions and <u>underline</u> the key information.

2 Susie wants to buy her friend a birthday present but she is short of time. She often gets her earrings, so she's thinking of getting her a top, perhaps something recycled with a pattern.

3 Mo's mum is about to go on a trip for work and he'd like to get her something useful which isn't another bag. He needs to be able to take it back if she doesn't like it.

4 Lucas urgently needs something for his school stuff. The zip on his last bag broke, so he's looking for something stronger with room for a tracksuit for when he does training.

5 Lizzie would like to buy something for a fancy-dress party. Last year she dressed up as a clown, so she'd like something different that's easy to do up.

4 Read the guide to eight market stalls. Decide which stall would be the most suitable for the people in Exercise 3.

EXAM TIP

Read the descriptions and <u>underline</u> the key information. Match this key information with one of the longer descriptions (A–H). All the key information needs to appear in the correct answer.

Going to the market?
HERE ARE EIGHT OF OUR FAVOURITE STALLS!

A MARTHA'S GOODIES 🔊 1.2

Martha's got an amazing range of necklaces and bracelets on display and she'll let you try on everything. We particularly like her gold chains and earrings with coloured stones. They aren't cheap, but they'd make the perfect gift to celebrate a special occasion. Open from midday every day.

B COOL THINGS

At the Cool Things stall, you'll find all kinds of accessories, including unusual rings and earrings made of all different kinds of metal. Rapper Joe D's responsible for the original designs. With affordable prices, there's something to suit all tastes. They're open from Wednesday to Sunday.

C JAKE'S DESIGNS

Voted Stall of the Month, bring your picture and Jake and his team will turn it into a creative piece of clothing. At busy times, allow about an hour for Jake to do his magic but the wait will be worth it. Located at the front gate, you can't miss it! No returns!

D DINAH'S DEN

They've got an amazing collection of leather goods of all sizes for work or for pleasure. Just arrived: high-quality rucksacks which will last for years! You'll never need to replace them. Changed your mind? No problem, return it within 30 days for a full refund.

E TREASURE BOX

Come and explore this huge selection of second-hand goods. There's something for everyone, from hats to socks and from T-shirts to skirts, with flowers or without! What's more, tell Kai what you're looking for and he'll find it within minutes!

F WE'VE GOT YOU COVERED!

Are you going on a trip? Are you looking for a bargain? Look no further! This stall sells last year's travel goods including suitcases, walking shoes, boots and rain jackets all at unbelievable prices! Please note that all sales are final and no returns are allowed!

G SAM'S STALL

Another recycled clothes stall is Sam's stall. Sit down with Sam for a cup of tea and a chat about what you need. Then he'll help you find the perfect costume for that special occasion. Need something changed? He can replace buttons with zips or remove them completely.

H ELLIE'S BAZAAR

Looking for a special gift? Ellie's purses and wallets are made of high-quality Italian leather and come in black or brown. She'll even put your initials on it for a small fee. Not happy with your purchase? You can return all non-personalised items.

PRESENT SIMPLE AND PRESENT CONTINUOUS

1 Watch the grammar vlog. Whose clothes do you like the best? Why?

▶ 02

2 Complete the grammar rules with the present simple or present continuous.

Present simple and present continuous

1 We use the _____ to talk about something that:
- happens regularly (and routines).
- is generally true and permanent.

2 We use the _____ to talk about something that:
- is happening at the moment or some time in the present.
- is temporary.

▶ Grammar reference and practice page 114

---

3 🖥 Go to the digital activities.

♻ **4** Complete the text with the present simple or present continuous form of the verbs in brackets.

Red N●se Day

Every two years, people across the UK ¹ _____ (celebrate) Red Nose Day in March. Why this name? It's because people ² _____ (usually / put on) red noses and ³ _____ (do) silly things. For example, around 90% of all secondary school children in the UK have to wear a school uniform. Most of us ⁴ _____ (not like) wearing one. However, today, as it ⁵ _____ (be) Red Nose Day, we ⁶ _____ (not wear) our uniforms but our teachers ⁷ _____ (wear) one! We ⁸ _____ (have) so much fun! It's hilarious. This year, my school ⁹ _____ (raise) money for a children's charity. ¹⁰ _____ you ever _____ (do) silly things for charity?

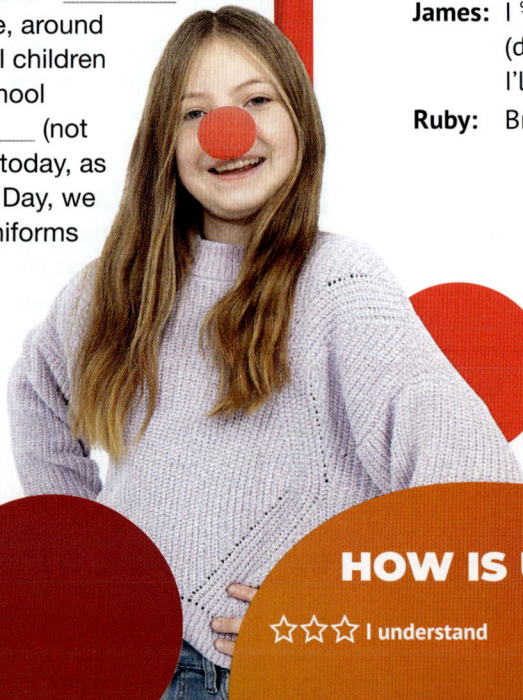

5 Choose the correct words to complete the grammar rules.

State verbs

State verbs talk about a state or condition, and they are not usually used in the ¹ *present simple / present continuous*. Here are some common ² *state / action* verbs.

believe depend have hope know like look love need prefer see seem suppose think understand want wish

Some verbs can be both state verbs and action verbs, but they have ³ *the same / a different* meaning.

A: Why are you looking in my wardrobe? Do you want to borrow something? (*looking* = directing your eyes at something)

B: Wow! You look great in that costume. (*look* = appear)

---

6 🖥 PRONUNCIATION Go to the digital pronunciation activity.

7 Complete the conversation with the correct present simple or present continuous form of the verbs in brackets.

Ruby: ¹ _____ we _____ (have) a Red Nose Day at school again this year?

James: I ² _____ (think) so. I ³ _____ (need) to find something to wear.

Ruby: I ⁴ _____ (not understand). Why?

James: Well, I ⁵ _____ (look) for something smart for non-uniform day.

Ruby: I ⁶ _____ (see)! What ⁷ _____ you _____ (plan) on wearing? The new charity shop next to the cinema ⁸ _____ (look) cool. How about going there on Saturday? Are you free?

James: I ⁹ _____ (hope) so but it ¹⁰ _____ (depend) on my mum. If she has to work, I'll need to look after my little brother.

Ruby: Bring him along too!

HOW IS UNIT 1 SO FAR?

☆☆☆ I understand   ☆☆ I'm getting there   ☆ I don't understand

WE WANT A **UNIFORM**!

Eddie and Sora went to school in England for a year. Here, Eddie tells us how his opinion about school uniforms has changed.

When Sora and I started at our English school, we didn't like the uniform. Sora had to wear a heavy woollen skirt and I had a formal shirt and a striped tie. It was uncomfortable! My trousers felt too baggy and my shirt felt too tight. At first we thought that English schools were old-fashioned, but then we learned that school uniforms are common all over the world. Students wear them in most of Asia, most African countries and many other countries … so why not here in the US?

We've all felt the pressure to have trendy clothes if we want to fit in at school. Parents often complain that we want overpriced things, but the better-value options are not cool. Uniforms solve that problem. Nobody in a uniform will be bullied for having unfashionable clothes. It should save money, though I've also read that in some places children can't go to school because they can't afford the uniform. School uniforms should be free!

Believe Sora and me: it's *great* when you don't have to think about what to put on in the morning. I didn't like our woollen trousers in England, though. A light cotton outfit would be more practical for our warm climate here in California. Well, Sora says she wants a gorgeous green silk blouse, but maybe that's not quite realistic!

We know that most people at our school will say 'no' when asked if they want a uniform. But think about it: It has some real advantages.

MEDIATION WORKSHEET

READING

AN ARTICLE

1 Read the headline in the article. In pairs, make a list of good things about school uniforms.

2 Skim the article. Tick (✓) the ideas in your list which are mentioned.

3 ◁) 1.3 Read the article again and listen. Answer the questions in your own words.

  1 How did Eddie and Sora feel about their English school uniform at first?

  2 According to Eddie, what do parents often think about the clothes that teenagers want?

  3 How could uniforms stop some people from going to school?

  4 Do Eddie and Sora expect students at their school to be enthusiastic about uniforms?

4 **Creative Thinking** What are the disadvantages of school uniforms? In groups, brainstorm reasons why it could be better not to have one.

VOCABULARY

ADJECTIVES TO DESCRIBE CLOTHES

1 ◁) 1.4 Put each of the adjectives in the right category. Listen, check and repeat.

baggy cotton gorgeous silk striped tight
trendy uncomfortable unfashionable woollen

Opinion	Shape, size, patterns	Material

2 ◁) 1.5 Go to the digital activity and match the phrases to the photos. Listen, check and repeat.

a baggy jumper a cotton T-shirt a silk dress
a striped shirt a woollen jumper tight jeans

▶ Vocabulary reference page 16

3 In pairs, write two sentences to describe the clothes in each picture in Exercise 2. Use the words from Exercise 1, including the opinion words, and your own ideas.

4 Show your descriptions from Exercise 3 to another pair. Did you write the same things?

ORACY

Giving encouragement

It's nice to pay people compliments if they have new clothes or accessories, or if you see them wearing something that you like.

5 ◁) 1.6 Listen to two friends at a party. What three phrases do they use to pay each other compliments?

You look great today.

6 Turn to your partner and pay him or her a compliment.

GRAMMAR
ADJECTIVES: WORD ORDER

1 Watch the grammar animation. Hassan and Rebecca are planning to go to a fancy-dress party. What is Rebecca's costume?

▶ 03

2 Look at the example and put the words in the correct order.

> **Adjectives: word order**
>
> *I love my wonderful, big, old, square, blue, Australian leather bag!*
>
> > age   colour   material   ~~opinion~~
> > origin (place)   shape   size
>
> When more than one adjective comes before a noun, they generally come in this order:
>
> _____opinion_____ , _____ ,
>
> _____ , _____ ,
>
> _____ , _____ ,
>
> _____ noun
>
> We do not usually use more than three adjectives before a noun.
>
> ▶ Grammar reference and practice page 114

3 🖥 Go to the digital activities.

4 Ben and his mother went shopping for clothes yesterday. Complete the text with the words in the correct order.

Yesterday, Mum and I went shopping in a(n) ^1 _____ (big / interesting / shop). You can get ^2 _____ (cool / clothes / new) direct from the factory, so it's not expensive. I got a ^3 _____ (jumper / woollen / lovely) there. My mum got a ^4 _____ (nice / cotton / blue / dress). Then we went for a ^5 _____ (Chinese / delicious / lunch). They served the food in ^6 _____ (modern / bowls / huge / round). It looked great!

>>> STRETCH! In some languages you can leave out the noun after the adjective. We don't usually do this in English. We don't say: ~~What a cute!~~ or ~~What cute!~~ We say: *What a cute baby!* **Find more examples of adjectives used without nouns.**

DIGITAL CLASSROOM
PRACTICE EXTRA UNIT 1

SPEAKING
DESCRIBING A PHOTO

1 🔊 1.7 Listen to a candidate describe this picture in Part 2 of the Speaking exam. What adjectives did he use?

ORACY

Giving yourself thinking time

Sometimes you need to keep talking but aren't sure exactly what you want to say. Don't leave long gaps. Give yourself thinking time using phrases like *Well, anyway … / Hmm, where can this be? / So, what else can I tell you?*

2 🔊 1.7 Listen to the candidate from Exercise 1 again. Which thinking time phrases from the oracy box does he use?

☑ **EXAM TASK** SPEAKING PART 2

EXAM TIP

> When you describe a photo, talk about everything you can see: the people, clothes, the place, etc. Use adjectives to add to the description and say where things are.

3 Work in pairs. Student A, look at photo A on page 124.

4 Student B, listen to your partner and then give feedback using this checklist.

Did your partner:
- describe the people?
- describe the place?
- keep going, using thinking time phrases?
- use adjectives?
- say where things are?

5 Swap roles. Student B, look at photo B on page 125.

CHALLENGE — 1 2 3 4

Develop

1   In your groups, talk about or show each other websites you have seen and like.
2   Decide what ideas you can use to design your own website and whether you want to use one website as a model or use a mix of ideas.
3   Design some pages which you can show to your classmates. You can use paper or digital options if you have them.
4   Create a first draft of your website.

WRITING

A FLYER

1   Look at the title and photo in the flyer. What do you think it advertises?

EVERY SECOND SUNDAY!

One person's rubbish is another person's gold!

Is your home full of unwanted junk? At our flea market, you can sell or swap your second-hand stuff. Clothes, accessories, books and music are always popular, but feel free to bring anything you can carry. (No animals though, please!) Or perhaps you're looking for an unusual gift. Come along and have a look at what's on sale!

The market takes place on the first and third Sunday of every month just behind the sports centre. If you're selling, you'll need to book a stall in advance (€10) and there's a small entrance fee for shoppers (€5), but this money goes to local mental health charities.

Let's give our old things a new life! Just remember, your rubbish might be someone else's gold!

Check our website for more information!

www.everysecondsunday.org

---

2   Read the flyer. Would you like to go to the market? Why? / Why not?

3   Look at the flyer again and find an example of each of these things. In what order do they appear?

   a   a website address
   b   information about the date, time, location, etc.
   c   information about what you can buy
   d   a title and subtitle
   e   a photo or illustration
   f   a call to action

4   Work in pairs. Answer the questions.

   1   Why is the market called 'Every second Sunday'?
   2   What do you think 'One person's rubbish is another person's gold!' means?
   3   Why does the writer use questions in the text?
   4   What words does the writer use to encourage the reader to take action?

5   Read the task. What do you need to design? What information do you need to include?

> Your school would like to organise a second-hand market to raise money for a local charity. It has invited students to design the flyer and will choose the best one. The winning flyer should include the following:
>
> • an attractive title
> • a photo or illustration
> • information about the market (what's on sale, date, time, location and cost)
> • a call to action
> • a website address

6   Design your flyer, including all the information in Exercise 5. Use some of the words and expressions from the model flyer.

7   Read your flyer again and revise your work. Use these questions to help you.

   1   Does the flyer look attractive?
   2   Is all the information from the task included?
   3   Does the flyer include some of the words and expressions from the model and from this unit?
   4   Can you see any problems with the language?

8   **Learning to Learn**   Now work in pairs. Read each other's flyers and give feedback. Use the questions in Exercise 7 to help you. Make a note of your partner's feedback and write a second draft of your flyer.

9   Display the flyers on the classroom walls. Which one do you think the school should use? Why?

10   Read the model answer.

LISTENING

SHORT MONOLOGUE OR DIALOGUE

1 Read the question and <u>underline</u> the key words.

1 What does the boy decide to buy?

A   B   C

2 Look at the pictures in Exercise 1 again. What different words can you use to describe each one?

3 🔊 1.8 Listen to the conversation. Choose the correct answer (A, B or C) in Exercise 1.

EXAM TIP
You will always listen to the recording twice. Use the second time you listen to check your work and also to write down any missing answers.

✓ EXAM TASK LISTENING PART 1

4 🔊 1.9 <u>Underline</u> the key words in questions 2–7 and look at the pictures.
Then listen to the rest of the conversations. For each question, choose the correct answer.

2 What is the boy doing?

A   B   C

3 What's on TV later?

A   B   C

4 Where did the girl leave her phone?

A   B   C

5 What's the problem with the hoodie?

A   B   C

6 Where will the friends go next?

A   B   C

7 Where did the boy get his belt?

A   B   C

5 🔊 1.9 Listen again and check your answers.

ORACY

Organising your answer

When you answer a friend's question with a story, use words like 'It's a long story', 'but then ...' and 'eventually'.

6 🔊 1.10 In question 7 in the Exam Task, the girl asks the boy, 'Where did you get that belt?' Listen to and read his answer. What words does he use to structure his answer?

It's a long story. I spent ages looking around the shops in town, but they didn't have anything suitable. Dad then suggested I look around that trendy second-hand market on Peter Street, but none of them were very nice. Eventually I found one online, but it didn't last long. My uncle's neighbour mends shoes, so he managed to repair it and it's great!

7 Work in pairs. Take turns to ask and answer 'Where did you get your ...?' Remember to structure your answer.

🛡 CHALLENGE ❶❷❸❹

Present

1 Make sure you have everything for your presentation.

2 Check that everyone in your group knows their roles.

3 Present your website to your class.

4 During the presentations, write down two or three questions. Ask them at the end.

WRAP UP

Look back at the unit. Write down:

1. some new vocabulary you learned to talk about clothes.
2. your main role in the challenge.
3. one use of the present continuous.
4. a sentence describing a coat, with three adjectives.
5. something in the unit that you especially enjoyed.

⟳ Sustainability

1 Think of a sustainable way you can get great clothes without going to a clothes shop.

2 How is it sustainable?

SELF-ASSESSMENT: UNIT 1

How confident do you feel about:

- finding key information in short written texts?
- finding key information in short monologues and dialogues?
- describing a photograph?
- designing and writing a flyer?
- using the present simple and present continuous?
- using adjectives in the right order before nouns?
- using words for naming and describing clothes?
- presenting a website to your classmates?

What was your favourite part of Unit 1? Tell your partner.

🖳 **Digital Literacy** Look back at Unit 1, page 8, Exercise 7. What words in your search produced better results? Why?

⟫ STRETCH! YOUR CHOICE

Now, choose an option.

Option 1:
Find a website that you think is really useful, and that is *not* about clothes. Tell your classmates about it. Say what information it gives you and why you think it is good.

Option 2:
Imagine your school is introducing a uniform (or a *new* uniform if you already have one). Design it! Draw it on paper or use a website that lets you create uniforms. Present your design to the class.

Option 3:
Have a fancy-dress party in your next English lesson. Ask everyone to wear a costume and to describe the costume and explain why they chose it to the rest of the class.

VOCABULARY REFERENCE

CLOTHES

1 Match the words to the photos.

buttons   costume   jersey   laces   material   pattern   sleeves   sweatshirt   tracksuit   zip

ADJECTIVES TO DESCRIBE CLOTHES

2 Look at the photos and use one or two of the adjectives to describe each one.

baggy   cotton   gorgeous   silk   striped   tight
trendy   uncomfortable   unfashionable   woollen

UNIT 2 FREE TIME

LEARNING AIMS

- **Skills:** discuss and create texts about free-time activities
- **Grammar:** learn and practise past simple, past continuous, past perfect and adverbs of sequence
- **Vocabulary:** learn and practise words and phrases for hobbies and leisure, and entertainment and media
- **Oracy:** give a presentation
- **Exam practice:** Reading Part 1, Writing Part 2, Listening Part 2

ORACY

Giving a presentation
- speaking clearly and at an appropriate speed
- using humour
- making positive comments and asking sensible questions

1 **Look at the photo. Discuss the questions in small groups.**

1 What can you see?
2 How do the people feel?
3 Some people say that young people have too much free time. Do you agree?

2 **Watch the video and answer the questions.**

1 What are the benefits of taking up a hobby?
2 What different hobbies do you see?
3 Which of the activities would you like to try? Which would you not like to try? Why?

▶ 01

3 **In small groups, play Just a Minute. Each person talks about one of these topics for a minute without pausing or stopping.**

- Everyone should take up a hobby.
- Parents and teachers should decide how young people spend their free time.
- Everyone should spend some time doing voluntary work in their free time.
- Resting in your free time is a waste of time.

4 **Think about your mini presentations in Exercise 3. Did you use any of the skills in the Oracy box? Which ones? Compare your answers.**

Documentary

Grammar

Grammar

Oracy

VOCABULARY

HOBBIES AND LEISURE

1 🔊 **2.1 Go to the digital activity and match the words to the photos. Listen, check and repeat.**

draw cartoons   go hiking
go out on my bike   hang out with friends
perform on stage   start a collection
have a barbecue   try out new recipes

▶ **Vocabulary reference page 26**

2 **PRONUNCIATION** **Go to the digital pronunciation activity.**

3 **Read these descriptions of people. Which would be the best activity in Exercise 1 for each person?**

1   Robbie's keen on spending time in the open air with friends and keeping fit, but he isn't into cycling at all.

2   Yasmin's crazy about music and goes to concerts whenever she can. She keeps all the tickets but isn't sure about what to do with them.

3   Ali enjoys making his friends laugh and they think he could take part in a comedy show.

4   Lara has always been fond of art. She often enters competitions but would like to take up something a little different which is still art.

5   Alex is tired of making the same dishes every week. He's ready for a change.

4 **Read these questions and copy the expressions with *take*. Then ask and answer the questions in pairs.**

1   When was the last time you took up something new? What was it?

2   How often do you take part in competitions?

3   Why is it important to take a rest?

4   Do you and your family take turns to choose a programme on TV?

5   How often do exciting events take place in your town?

6   Do you do things quickly or do you take your time?

7   How do you take advantage of a long weekend?

8   What is the latest craze to take off?

>>> **STRETCH!** **In a speaking exam, the examiner may ask you about your hobbies, likes and dislikes. Make a list of all the things you (and the people you know) do in your free time and make sure you know how to say them in English.**

ORACY

Speaking clearly and at an appropriate speed

When we get nervous, we often speak too quickly and our audience may not be able to understand us. Before you start speaking, take a few deep, full breaths from your stomach and then begin.

5 🔊 **2.2 You are going to listen to a relaxation exercise. Listen to the recording and follow the teacher's instructions.**

6 **Discuss the questions with a partner and reflect on Exercise 5.**

1   How did you feel during the relaxation? How did you feel after?

2   Why might it be useful to do a relaxation exercise before giving a presentation?

3   When else might this relaxation exercise be useful? Think of at least two more situations.

7 **You are going to give a short presentation on a hobby or activity. Choose one from this unit or use your own idea. Make some notes by answering these questions.**

1   What is the activity? How do you do it?

2   What equipment do you need?

3   What are the benefits of doing it?

8 **Work with a partner. Student A, present your hobby or activity from your notes in Exercise 7. Student B, listen and give Student A some feedback using the questions below to help. Then swap roles.**

1   Did your partner take some deep breaths before starting?

2   Did your partner speak clearly and slowly?

3   Did you understand your partner?

READING

REAL WORLD NOTICES

1 Look at the real-world notices. Where would you find each one?

◁)) 2.3

1

FOR SALE

Brand new judo suit still unwrapped.

Received as a gift but too big and can't be returned.

Please contact harry@harry.com for more information.

A The judo suit was bought online.
B The judo suit fits the owner well.
C The judo suit has never been used.

2 ← **Zak**
Online

Greg,

Comic-Con takes place this weekend. Fancy taking part in the cartoon-drawing competition with me?

I'll check the details and get back to you.

Zak

A Zak asks Greg to find out some information.
B Zak would like to enter a contest with Greg.
C Zak wants Greg to make him a comic.

3 **From:** Concert Hall   **To:** Customers

Due to heavy storms, tonight's open-air concert has been cancelled. Please contact the organiser directly for a full refund. We apologise for any disappointment.

A Some people have complained about the musicians.
B You can get your money back for your ticket.
C The weather will be better tomorrow.

4 *Art Gallery Holiday*

We're taking a week's break from Monday. We'll have a special show on the following Saturday plus a brand-new photography course for under-18s.

A The art gallery will be open on Monday.
B Everyone can learn how to take better photos.
C A different exhibition will be on next weekend.

5 **DRAMA SOCIETY**

Actors, directors and designers welcome! Sign up early to book a place as this is one of the most popular clubs.

A If you want to join, tell us as soon as possible.
B We regret to say that the drama club is now full.
C All kinds of people run the club.

2 Read the notices more carefully and also read the answers. <u>Underline</u> the key words.

EXAM TASK READING PART 1

EXAM TIP

Answer each question one by one. First read the notice carefully and underline the key words. Next read the answers A–C and underline the key words. Make sure you understand the difference between each option before you read the text again to find the correct answer. Once you have answered all the questions, go back and check your work.

3 Now choose the correct answers.

4 Some people say that young people should take part in several different after-school activities. In small groups, talk about whether you agree or disagree.

GRAMMAR

PAST SIMPLE AND PAST CONTINUOUS

1 Watch the grammar vlog. Who's Marek? What did he do?

▶ 02

2 Complete the grammar rules with *past simple* or *past continuous*.

> **Past simple and past continuous**
>
> 1 We use the _____ to talk about actions or situations in the past (often one action happened after the other).
> 2 We use the _____ to talk about an activity that was already happening at a moment in the past.
> 3 We use the _____ to show an action that interrupted or happened in the middle of a _____ activity.
>
> ▶ Grammar reference and practice page 115

3 🖥 Go to the digital activities.

4 Complete the conversation with the verbs in brackets in the past simple or past continuous.

Lee: How ¹ _____ the family barbecue in the park _____ (go) on Saturday?

Mia: We ² _____ (have) a lot of fun, but something really embarrassing ³ _____ (happen). While we ⁴ _____ (finish) our burgers, a woman ⁵ _____ (start) shouting, 'Who wants some fruit?'

Lee: ⁶ _____ she _____ (give) it away for free?

Mia: Well, she ⁷ _____ (have) a huge box so I ⁸ _____ (run) over to her. About six other people ⁹ _____ (wait) in the queue. When I ¹⁰ _____ (reach) the front, the woman ¹¹ _____ (look) at me and ¹² _____ (ask), 'Who are you?'

Lee: Oh no! What ¹³ _____ you _____ (say)?

5 Complete the rules with *when* or *while*.

> **When or while?**
>
> 1 We generally use _____ before an action in the past simple.
> 2 We can use _____ and _____ before an activity in the past continuous.
>
> ▶ Grammar reference and practice page 115

6 Read these pairs of sentences. What is the difference in meaning between them?

1 a When I arrived, everyone was playing cards.
   b When I arrived, everyone played cards.
2 a While I was watching TV, my brother was drawing a cartoon.
   b While I was watching TV, my brother drew a cartoon.
3 a I was riding my bike when it started to rain.
   b I was riding my bike while it was raining.

7 Make some notes in the past simple and past continuous about a recent weekend. Include three lies.

8 Work in pairs. Take turns to ask and answer questions in the past simple and past continuous about a recent weekend. Can you find the three lies?

⟫⟫ STRETCH! People often talk about important events and say things like 'When my country won the World Cup, I was watching the match at home.' Find out about an important event in your country and find out what the people you know were doing at the time.

HOW IS UNIT 2 SO FAR?

☆☆☆ I understand   ☆☆ I'm getting there   ☆ I don't understand

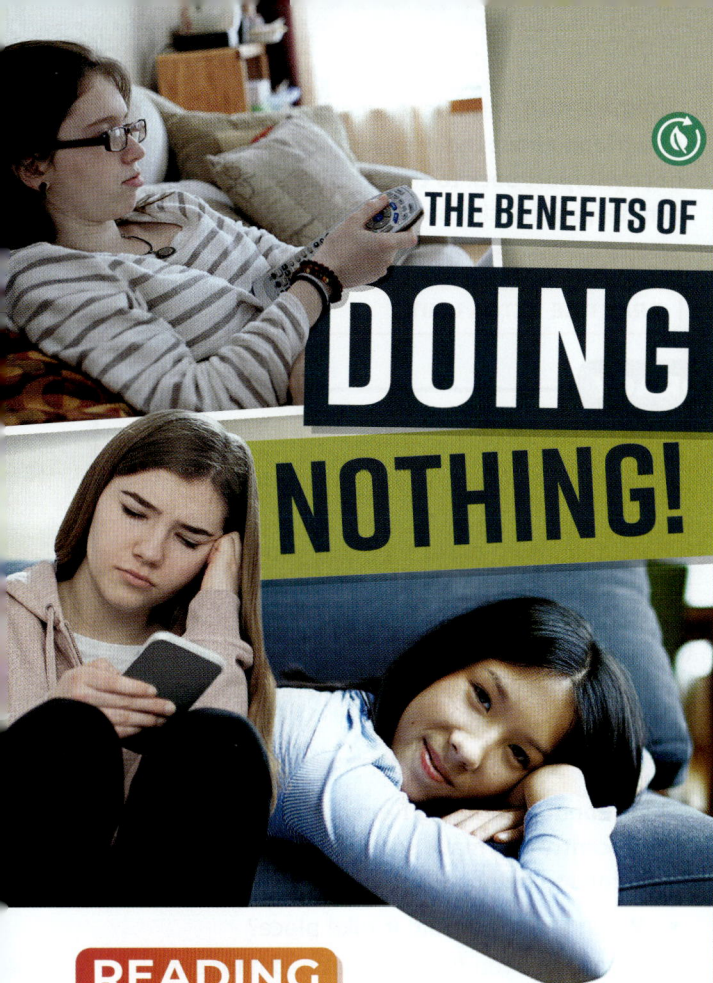

THE BENEFITS OF DOING NOTHING!

My friend Viola ran the school newspaper and had also signed up for music lessons. She was a DJ at her friends' parties and a regular blogger. When the cycling team approached her about a race last Sunday, she felt she couldn't say no, even though she was exhausted and just wanted to do nothing. Research shows that doing nothing at some point in our week is good for the health of our brains.

Yet, if you think that looking at your phone is a good way of doing nothing, think again! Studies show that we are now spending twice as much time on our screens than just a few years ago. Perhaps we're downloading a video clip, uploading a photo onto social media or even catching up with friends online or the latest TV series. Concentrating for too long on the screen isn't good for us! It can cause tired eyes and 'tech neck', which is neckache after using technology for too long.

So am I suggesting **NO** activity? Actually, no! In fact, a recent report suggests that sitting around for long periods, doing nothing at all, can cause depression. Doing as little as 60 minutes of light, stress-free activity such as going for a walk can reduce this risk. That said, a quick afternoon sleep on the sofa can also help our minds (and our bodies) recover.

So, what's the key? Find your own out-of-school balance! Limit your screen time to two hours a day, add a stress-free activity to your week, and then sit on the sofa. Close your eyes for 15 minutes and do nothing!

READING

AN ARTICLE

1 **Work in pairs. Look at the title of the article and the photo. What do you think 'doing nothing' involves? How often do you 'do nothing'?**

2 🔊 **2.4 Read and listen to the article and check your ideas in Exercise 1.**

3 **Are the sentences true or false? Correct the false sentences.**

1 Viola was delighted to take part in the cycling competition.

2 Experts say that it isn't good to be active all the time.

3 Young people get 'tech neck' if they spend too much time on their homework.

4 It's OK to do absolutely nothing all day.

5 Doing an hour's activity a day can improve our mental health.

6 The writer suggests that we shouldn't spend more than two hours a day on our phones.

4 🎯 Creative Thinking **Work in pairs. Choose one of these situations and decide on your role. Discuss the situation calmly with your partner and try to reach an agreement.**

1 A teacher wants to set some extra homework. The student is tired.

2 A teenager wants to go to an event in another town. The parent is too tired to drive.

3 Friend A wants to go out and do something active. Friend B wants to stay in and chill out.

VOCABULARY

ENTERTAINMENT AND MEDIA

1 💻 🔊 **2.5 Go to the digital activity and match the collocations to the photos. Listen, check and repeat.**

be a blogger   be a DJ
catch up with a TV series
check social media   download a video clip
run a newspaper   sign up for lessons
upload a photo

▶ **Vocabulary reference page 26**

2 **Work in pairs. What do you think? Decide which of the activities in Exercise 1 are:**

- a waste of time
- a good way to relax
- a good use of time
- stressful

3 **Work in small groups. Students from another country are coming to your town. Plan a week's programme of both active and more relaxing activities.**

>>> STRETCH! Find at least two more nouns that go with these verbs: *catch up with*, *check*, *download*, *run*, *sign up for* **and** *upload*.

GRAMMAR
PAST PERFECT

1 Watch the grammar animation. What happened to Rebecca and Hassan?

▶ 03

2 Complete the sentences from the grammar animation. Watch again and check.

1 I _____ the folk dancing club and this was our first performance.
2 Well, she was trying to tell me I _____ her dance shoes.
3 I realised they _____ a mistake.

3 Choose the correct words to complete the grammar rule.

> **Past perfect**
> We use the past perfect to describe something which happened **before / after** another action or event in the past.
> *When I **got** to school, I **realised** that I **had left** my bag on the bus.*
>
> ▶ Grammar reference and practice page 115

4 🖥 Go to the digital activities.

5 Complete the article with the correct past simple, past continuous or past perfect form of the verbs in brackets.

… 🔍

LOCAL NEWS   WORLD NEWS   BUSINESS   POLITICS

Mason Bevan becomes young ballroom dancing star!

When Mason Bevan [1] _____ (be) just four years old, a local dance group [2] _____ (perform) at his school. Soon after, Mason [3] _____ (sign up) for ballroom dancing lessons. While other children [4] _____ (play) computer games at home, Mason [5] _____ (learn) to dance. His older brother [6] _____ also _____ (be) a dancer but he [7] _____ it _____ (give up) and [8] _____ (take up) rugby instead. By the age of 12, Mason [9] _____ (become) the UK Juvenile Ballroom and Latin Champion and he [10] _____ (win) a championship in Germany. At 17, he [11] _____ already _____ (appear) on *Strictly Come Dancing*, a British TV show, and he [12] _____ (begin) to take part in competitions for adults.

👥 MEDIATION WORKSHEET

>>> STRETCH! Interview a member of your family or a friend about their reasons for taking up a hobby. Report back to the class using the past simple, past continuous and past perfect.

DIGITAL CLASSROOM ▶
PRACTICE EXTRA UNIT 2

ORACY

Using humour
Presenters sometimes use funny stories and jokes to make their talks more interesting. However, before doing this, make sure that your audience will understand the story or joke and that it does not make anyone upset or angry. Then, when you're telling your story, pause before your punchline, look at your audience and use a different voice to deliver it.

6 Think about something funny that happened to you recently and make some notes. Use these questions to help you.

- When and where did it take place?
- What were you doing? What had happened before? What happened next?
- What happened at the end? What's your punchline?

7 Work in small groups. Take turns to tell your story from Exercise 6. Use these tips to help you.

- Vary your voice by speaking higher or lower, softer or louder, etc.
- Pause before you deliver the punchline.
- Make a funny face at the end of the story to make people laugh.

8 🎓 Learning to Learn **Evaluate your performance. Answer the questions.**

- Did you speak clearly and slowly?
- Was the group interested in your story? Did they find it funny?
- How do you know?

WRITING

A STORY

1 Look at the photo. What is the woman doing?

2 Read the story and choose the best first sentence.

1 I got on the bus and sat down next to someone I knew.

2 I was walking home when I heard someone call my name.

3 My phone rang just as I was leaving school.

It was my friend Nikki. She was obviously crying so I asked her what was wrong. ¹ _____ she didn't want to tell me but ² _____ she explained that she had borrowed her brother's camera and she had lost it. ³ _____ she was doing parkour in the park, she was keeping it on a bench. ⁴ _____, it wasn't there. I decided to go and meet her to help look for it. ⁵ _____ several hours, we still hadn't found it. ⁶ _____ we were about to give up, Nikki's brother phoned. ⁷ _____, someone had found it and had called him.

3 Complete the story with the words in the box.

> after   at first   in the end   just as
> suddenly   then   while

4 Read the story again and put these events in order. What different past tenses does the narrator use to make the story more interesting?

a Nikki lost her brother's camera.

b The narrator met Nikki.

c Nikki went to the park to do parkour.

d Someone found the camera.

e Nikki's brother phoned her.

f Nikki started crying.

✓ EXAM TASK   WRITING PART 2

EXAM TIP

Use a range of past tenses (past simple, past continuous and past perfect) in your story to make it more interesting.

5 Read this exam task and write your story.

> Your English teacher has asked you to write a story. Your story must begin with this sentence.
>
> *I looked at my watch and decided it was too late to go in.*
>
> Write your **story**.

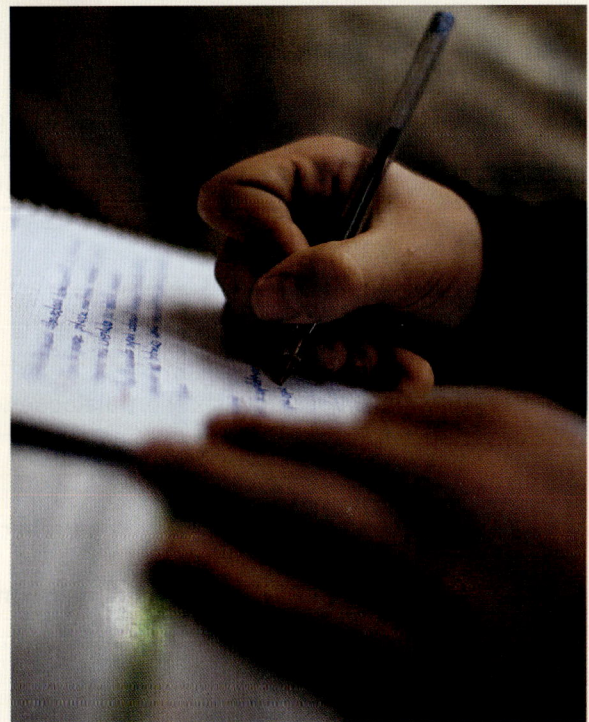

6 Read your story again and revise your work. Use these questions to help you.

1 Is the first line of the story the sentence from the exam task?

2 Is there a range of past tenses and vocabulary in the story?

3 Are there time words and phrases (*at first, after, suddenly*, etc.)?

4 Can you see any problems with the language (spelling, grammar, etc.)?

5 Is the story interesting and easy to follow?

7 Now work in pairs. Read each other's stories and give feedback. Use the questions in Exercise 6 to help you. Make a note of your partner's feedback and write a second draft of your story.

8 🖳 Read the model answer.

ORACY

GIVING A PRESENTATION

- speaking clearly and at an appropriate speed
- using humour
- making positive comments and asking sensible questions

1 ▶ 04 You are going to watch a video of some students planning a presentation. Which expressions do you hear?

You're right.	Maybe you should …
OK, I get your point.	I'm interested!
Cool! Awesome!	Can I (also) give you a piece of advice?

2 Next you will watch the students giving their presentation. Which of these things do you think you are going to see?

- a presenter (or team of presenters)
- presentation slides
- several interruptions
- time for comments and questions
- applause

3 Watch the video and check your ideas in Exercise 2.

▶ 05

ORACY

Making positive comments and asking sensible questions.

Some people find it stressful to present their ideas to others. Encourage them by saying positive things and asking questions at the end.

4 ▶ 06 How well do you think the group in the video did? Now watch the students evaluating their presentation and compare your ideas with theirs.

5 You are going to present an exciting programme of activities. Choose one of these events.

- the first day at school for new students
- an international camp
- a festival for young people

6 Plan your presentation.

- Choose the event and decide on an exciting programme of activities.
- Design the presentation slides and write the script. Involve your audience by including some humour and by asking two or three questions.
- Decide who is going to say what.
- Rehearse your presentation. Make sure that everyone speaks slowly and clearly.

7 Take turns to give your presentations. While you listen to the others, remember to make positive comments and ask questions at the end.

8 Discuss how well your presentation went using the oracy checklist. Complete the table.

	Me	My group
Speaking clearly and at an appropriate speed.		
Using humour.		
Making positive comments and asking sensible questions.		

SELF-ASSESSMENT: UNIT 2

How confident do you feel about:

- finding the main message in real-world notices?
- finding the main idea in short dialogues?
- speaking clearly and at an appropriate speed in a presentation?
- writing an interesting story?
- telling a personal story using the past simple, past continuous and past perfect?
- talking about hobbies and leisure, and entertainment and media?
- giving a presentation to your classmates?

What was your favourite part of Unit 2? Tell your partner.

☹ 😕 😐 🙂
☹ 😕 😐 🙂
☹ 😕 😐 🙂
☹ 😕 😐 🙂
☹ 😕 😐 🙂
☹ 😕 😐 🙂
☹ 😕 😐 🙂

DIGITAL CLASSROOM
PERSONALISED LEARNING

VOCABULARY REFERENCE

HOBBIES AND LEISURE

1 Match the words to the photos.

draw cartoons go hiking go out on my bike hang out with friends have a barbecue
perform on stage start a collection try out new recipes

ENTERTAINMENT AND MEDIA

2 Match the collocations to the photos.

be a blogger be a DJ catch up with a TV series check social media download a video clip
run a newspaper sign up for lessons upload a photo

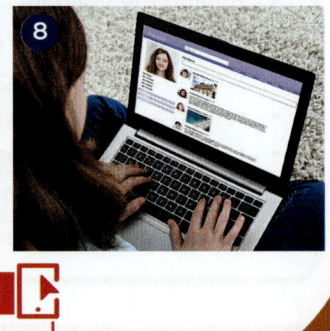

DIGITAL CLASSROOM
PRACTICE EXTRA UNIT 2

UNIT 3 THE NATURAL WORLD

LEARNING AIMS

- **Skills:** discuss and create texts about nature
- **Grammar:** learn and practise the present perfect, the past simple and *used to*
- **Vocabulary:** learn and practise words and phrases about animals and landscapes
- **Creative thinking:** find a solution to a loss of contact with nature
- **Exam practice:** Reading Part 3, Reading Part 6, Listening Part 3, Speaking Part 1

THE CHALLENGE

Young people have lost touch with nature.
You will:

- **Stage 1 Think:** find out about the positive aspects of spending time in nature.
- **Stage 2 Prepare:** find a way to bring more nature into your school.
- **Stage 3 Develop:** think about how to present your ideas.
- **Stage 4 Present:** try to persuade your classmates and/or teacher to take up your suggestions.

1 Look at the photo. Discuss the questions in small groups.

1 What can you see in the photo?
2 Where was the photo taken?
3 What are the advantages of having access to a garden?

2 Watch the video. What is a megacity? What are the advantages and disadvantages of living in one?

▶ 01

CHALLENGE ① ② ③ ④

Think

Discuss the questions with a partner and make notes.

1 How much time do you and your classmates spend in nature?
2 Would you be prepared to replace some of your screen time with wild time?
3 What kinds of things can you do in nature that you cannot do in a city?
4 What different things could we do to encourage more young people to get back in touch with nature?

Documentary

Grammar

Speaking

Grammar

VOCABULARY

ANIMALS

1 Work with a partner. Can you tell the difference between a bee and a wasp? What is it?

2 📱 🔊 **3.1** Go to the digital activity and match the words to the photos. Listen, check and repeat.

| bat | bee | deer | giraffe | goat | kangaroo |
| mosquito | owl | penguin | shark | wasp | zebra |

▶ Vocabulary reference page 36

3 Complete the table with the animals in Exercise 2.

Ocean	Farmland	Rainforest	Grassland	Icy region

4 Read the descriptions in the quiz and identify the animals. Use the words in Exercise 2.

Are you an a animal whizz or a goose?
Test yourself!

1 This animal has some interesting skills: it can run and climb, and when it has to defend itself, it can also kick, push and bite.

2 This animal uses its long neck to reach the best leaves at the top of trees or in bushes.

3 Both are insects, with black and yellow stripes and four wings. One appears to be softer and it makes honey.

4 This large fish can have up to 15 rows of sharp teeth.

5 Although this animal is more dangerous than a snake or a lion, only the female actually bites. Think about the diseases this insect carries.

6 This animal lives in the southern hemisphere. Scientists think there are 17–20 different species of this animal and the fastest can swim up to 35 km/hour.

5 Think back to the video on page 27. Why did the presenter mention these numbers?

> 56%   70%   10 million   80%   1 in 3
> 44%   19th century   21st century

6 ▶ 01 Watch the video again and check your ideas in Exercise 5.

7 Look at your answers in Exercise 5 again. Put an exclamation mark (!) next to the ones that surprise or shock you.

8 Now compare your answers with a partner and say why an answer surprises or shocks you.

9 🎓 **Creative Thinking** A teacher would like to teach a group of megacity kids more about animals and nature. Write down <u>at least two</u> interesting ways the teacher could do this. Don't be afraid to take risks with your ideas.

10 Now work in a small group. Listen to each other's ideas in Exercise 9 and evaluate them. Then work together to improve them.

CHALLENGE ─①②③④

Prepare

1 Form groups of three or four people.

2 Find out how different organisations are trying to bring young people back in touch with nature.

3 Make a list of possible ways you could bring nature into your school or classroom.

A SUMMER OF VOLUNTEERING

Seventeen-year-old Yana Novak talks about being a volunteer.   🔊 **3.2**

Over the summer, I got the chance to take part in a volunteer programme. Ever since I was a small child, I've always loved animals, but we weren't allowed to have pets when I was growing up. When I found out that I could work at a wildlife centre in Vancouver, Canada which rescues wild animals, I seized the opportunity. Named one of the most beautiful cities in the world, Vancouver is surrounded by nature. It has mountains on one side and the ocean on the other. It was definitely the best possible place for me!

The centre itself looks after sick and injured wild animals. I didn't realise this, but it is actually illegal for members of the public to care for them. The centre aims to help creatures like rabbits, deer and so on to get better so they can return to the wild. While I was staying there, one of the team brought in

READING

AN ARTICLE

1 Look at the photo. Would you like to work as a volunteer in a place like this?

2 Read the article and listen. Check your ideas in Exercise 1.

EXAM TIP

Remember that questions 1–4 follow the order of the text and each paragraph is tested. Question 5 focuses on the global meaning.

✓ EXAM TASK   READING PART 3

3 Read the questions. Work in pairs and try to answer them in your own words. Do NOT read the options for now.

1 Why has Yana Novak written the article?
   A to persuade people to visit Vancouver
   B to give advice on rescuing animals
   C to describe what the project involved
   D to explain why we should care for nature

2 What does Yana say about the wildlife centre?
   A It hopes that many animals will stay there forever.
   B It teaches animals how to survive in the wild.
   C It encourages the public to take care of wild animals.
   D It is located in a forest.

3 How did Yana feel about her work at the centre?
   A She was really tired because she worked too much.
   B She liked working at night best.
   C She felt pleased with what she had achieved.
   D She wanted to have more free time.

4 What advice does Yana give about applying to work at the centre?
   A Say why you are the most suitable person.
   B Take extra English classes before you go.
   C Make sure you send in your application form on time.
   D Wait until your 18th birthday before you apply.

5 What might Yana post on social media about her trip?
   A I had an amazing time looking after animals, but I wished the host family had offered me meals.
   B If I go back again next year, I'll certainly volunteer to work at night. That was enjoyable.
   C It was an unforgettable experience. The only thing I disliked was working every afternoon.
   D I'll never forget the trip. I've learned so much about penguins and other ocean animals.

4 For each question, choose the correct answer.

5 Read the text again and check your answers in Exercise 4.

6 Work in pairs. You are going to interview some candidates for a volunteer programme. Read the oracy tip and write some effective questions.

7 Now work in groups of three. Students A and B, interview Student C. Make some notes. Then change roles.

8 Look at your notes. Who should get the place?

ORACY

Asking questions

In an interview, ask different types of questions to get useful information. Start with easy questions like 'What do you do in your free time?' Then use open questions. 'What kind of contact have you had with animals?' is better than 'Have you worked with animals?'

a baby bat whose mum had died. I've learned that they're called pups! I learned to feed it with a bottle, being careful of its wings and making sure it didn't bite me. As it grew, we encouraged it to catch insects and spiders. Once it was ready, we took it out of the city and back into the forest.

I spent every morning at the centre, preparing food, cleaning out cages, doing the washing up and generally helping out. By the end of each session, I was exhausted but satisfied. I used to get the bus back to my host family, have lunch with them and fall asleep for an hour or so. We generally had the afternoons off. When we weren't hiking in the mountains or sailing around the port and islands, we were exploring the city. A couple of times, I asked if I could help overnight and that was so cool! Some of the animals such as the

mice, bats and owls are only completely awake at night.

For other animal lovers out there, the application process is fairly easy, but the minimum age for this programme is seventeen and you need a B1 Intermediate level of English. I used an online agency which helped me with the visa, flights, travel insurance and all the other details. You need to write a letter where you explain why you're the perfect candidate! I've wanted to work somewhere like this ever since I was young, so that part was easy for me. I've also taken up wildlife photography, so I added that in, too.

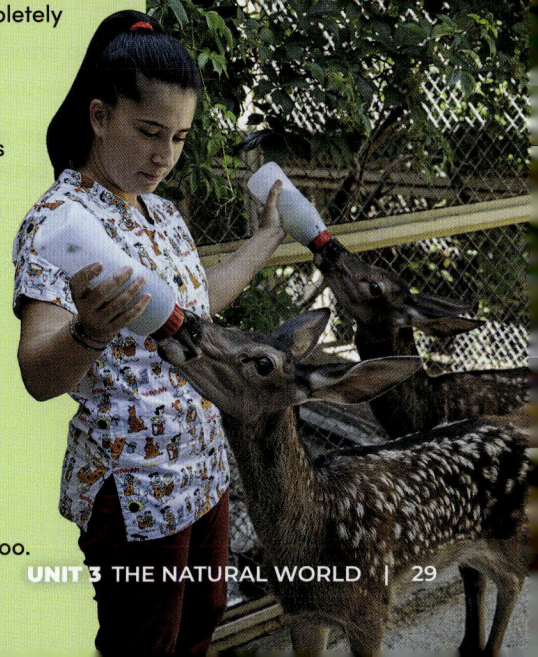

GRAMMAR

PRESENT PERFECT AND PAST SIMPLE

1 Watch the grammar animation. What do we learn about wallabies and kangaroos?

▶ 02

2 Complete the grammar rules with *present perfect* or *past simple*.

Present perfect and past simple

We use the _____ to talk about a past action:
- which has some link to the present.
- which happened in an unfinished time period.
- which started in the past and continues into the present.

We use the _____ to talk about a past action:
- when we say when it happened.
- which happened in a finished time period.
- which started and finished in the past.

▶ Grammar reference and practice page 116

3 💻 Go to the digital activities.

4 Complete the questions with the correct present perfect or past simple form of the verbs in brackets.

1 How long _____ (you / live) in this town?
2 Tell me about a friend. How _____ (you / meet) him/her?
3 When _____ (you / first get) a mobile phone?
4 Have you got a pet? How long _____ (you / have) it?

5 Work in pairs and ask and answer the questions in Exercise 4. Ask some follow-up questions.

>>> STRETCH! Find out about a national park. Write a short conversation between two people who visited it. Use the past simple and the present perfect.

SPEAKING

GIVING PERSONAL OR FACTUAL INFORMATION

1 You are going to watch an examiner asking Antonio and Lara some questions in Part 1 of the Speaking exam. Listen and write down the examiner's questions.

▶ 03

1 *What's your name?*

2 ▶ 03 Watch Antonio and Lara's answers carefully and answer the questions.

1 Do they listen to the examiner's questions carefully and give an appropriate answer?
2 Do they answer in full sentences?
3 Do they use the past simple and present perfect?

☑ EXAM TASK   SPEAKING PART 1

EXAM TIP

Listen carefully to the examiner's question and answer in complete sentences.

3 Work in pairs. Take turns to ask and answer the questions in Exercise 1. Listen to your partner and answer the questions.

- Does your partner listen carefully to your questions and give an appropriate answer?
- Does your partner answer in full sentences?

4 Give your partner some feedback. Use the questions in Exercise 3 to help you.

HOW IS UNIT 3 SO FAR?

☆☆☆ I understand   ☆☆ I'm getting there   ☆ I don't understand

LISTENING

DIALOGUES

1 In Part 2 of the exam, you will listen to two people giving their opinions on different things. Which of these expressions do you expect to hear?

> What do you think about ...?

> I think / believe / feel ...

> Don't you think so?

> I agree / disagree.

> That's true!

> That's awesome / cool / great!

2 Talk to a partner. Use the phrases in Exercise 1 to give your opinion on these things.

> an after-school club   a concert   a recent film   learning to play an instrument   social media

☑ EXAM TASK LISTENING PART 2

EXAM TIP

In this part, you will listen to six short dialogues. Make sure you read the first sentence of each question carefully as this will tell you what each dialogue is about.

3 Read questions 1–5 below carefully. What is each dialogue about?

4 ◁୬ 2.6 Listen to the recording. For each question, choose the correct answer.

1 You will hear two friends talking about a film they've seen. They agree that
  A the soundtrack was fantastic.
  B the special effects were awesome.
  C the actor's performance was excellent.

2 You will hear a boy talking to a friend about a concert. What does he say about it?
  A He got his ticket when he arrived.
  B The second part was disappointing.
  C There were too many people there.

3 You will hear a girl talking about a group on social media. What does she like best about it?
  A sharing amazing photos
  B discovering unusual dishes
  C discovering new websites

4 You will hear two friends talking about taking up a musical instrument. What does the boy advise the girl to do?
  A think about the cost of the instrument
  B play the same instrument as someone you know
  C choose something for classical music

5 You will hear two friends talking about a youth club. They both think it would be better if
  A there were fewer sports competitions.
  B it was in a bigger space.
  C they were involved in the decisions.

6 You will hear a girl telling her friend about being a DJ at a party. She felt
  A pleased to speak to different people.
  B hopeful of doing it again.
  C satisfied with her performance.

5 ◁୬ 2.6 Compare your answers with a partner and then listen again. (In the exam, you will hear each conversation twice before going on to the next question.)

LIVING IN A BIG CITY IS ACTUALLY GREENER!

Have you ever dreamed of living in a small cottage on top of a cliff with views over a sandy bay far away from a crowded city? It has to be more environmentally friendly, right? Think again! Experts have shown that large cities are often greener for a number of reasons. Let's explore them.

1 Cities fill less than 3% of the Earth. The fact that such a large population has decided to live in a small area means that we are not destroying nature. We don't spoil that gorgeous waterfall that flows into a stream and we can still go for long walks along the shore without meeting anyone.

2 People in cities usually live closer together in apartments. Providing essential services, such as heating and water, to one building is much more efficient than providing them to a tiny house in the valley.

3 On the whole, large cities offer a greater range of public transport so you would expect more pollution. Not really! As underground transport systems have grown in our cities, carbon dioxide levels have decreased. Another benefit, of course, is that people are more likely to use a well-developed transport system than a private car.

4 And finally, walkability! This is the ability to walk or cycle from your home to the local shops which sell locally produced products or to the mall which offers a variety of sustainable goods. This is not only better for the environment, but it's also great for your health.

So which do you choose? Will it be the romantic hut in the middle of the countryside or the city flat?

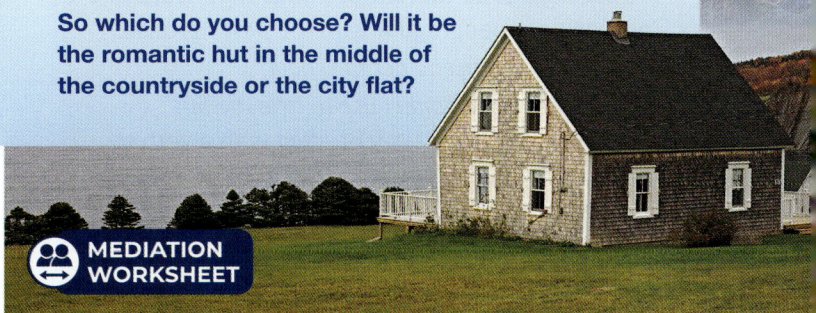

MEDIATION WORKSHEET

READING

AN ARTICLE

1 Work in pairs and answer the question.

Do you think living in a big city is greener than living in the countryside? Why? / Why not?

2 🔊 **3.3 Answer the questions. Then read the text and listen. Check your answers.**

1 How much of our planet is cities?
2 How does it save energy if we live in a block of flats?
3 How might a better transport system have less effect on climate change?
4 Why are people in a city less likely to use their own car?
5 What does the writer say about going places on foot?

3 🛡 **Critical Thinking** Work in pairs and look back at your answer in Exercise 1. Now that you have read the article, has your opinion changed? If so, say how.

VOCABULARY

LANDSCAPE

1 📷 🔊 **3.4 Go to the digital activity and match the landscape features to the photos. Listen, check and repeat.**

bay   canal   cave   cliff   coast
harbour   sand   shore   stream   valley

▶ Vocabulary reference page 36

2 Complete the diagram with the words in Exercise 1.

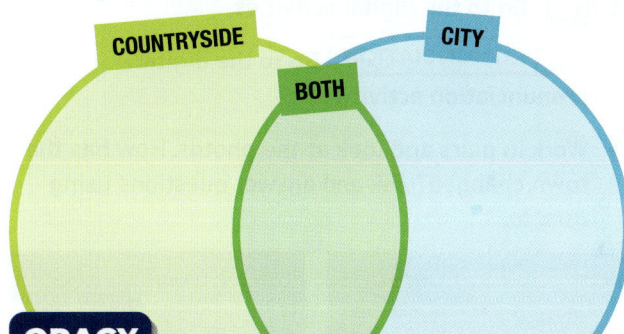

COUNTRYSIDE   CITY   BOTH

ORACY

Using a range of vocabulary

Remember to use a range of vocabulary and phrases to suit different situations.

3 Work in pairs. You work in the tourist office of a small village which would like to attract more people to the area. Complete the sentences with the words in Exercise 1 and your own ideas. Make sure you use a range of vocabulary.

1 If you like _____, I **suggest** you visit _____.
2 I **recommend** you take a walk along the _____ and **admire** the views over the _____.
3 **Consider / Try** going to down to the _____. You can _____ there.
4 I **urge** you to hire a boat _____. **You won't regret it!**

4 Work in small groups. Use your sentences in Exercise 3 to persuade each other to visit your village.

GRAMMAR
USED TO

1 Watch the grammar vlog. How have Leo's neighbourhood, town and school changed in the last five years?

▶ 04

2 Choose the correct words to complete the grammar rules.

> **used to**
>
> We use *used to* to talk about things that happened (or didn't happen) regularly in the *past / present*.
> *How did you use to get to school?*
> *I used to walk. I didn't use to take the bus.*
> We use words like *usually* or *often* with a verb to talk about regular actions in the *past / present*.
> *We often go for a walk along the cliffs at the weekend.*
>
> ▶ Grammar reference and practice page 116

3 🖥 Go to the digital activities.

4 🖥 [PRONUNCIATION] Go to the digital pronunciation activity.

5 Work in pairs and look at the photos. How has the town changed? Ask and answer questions using *used to*.

A: Did there use to be a lot of tall buildings here?

B: No, there didn't. Did this road used to be here?

A: No, it didn't.

▶▶▶ STRETCH! Find some old photos of your neighbourhood, town or school online. How has it changed? Report back to your classmates using *used to*.

DIGITAL CLASSROOM
PRACTICE EXTRA UNIT 3

READING
A SHORT TEXT

✓ **EXAM TASK** READING PART 6

EXAM TIP

Look at the words before and after the gap and decide what kind of word is missing. Is it a preposition, an auxiliary verb, an article or something else?

1 Read the text quickly, but do NOT complete the gaps for now. What is it about?

MARI COPENY 🔊 3.5

What ¹ _____ you use to want to be when you were younger? Sixteen-year-old Mari Copeny comes from Flint in Michigan, USA, and she would ² _____ to be president. Before 2014, their water used ³ _____ come from the main system and it was safe to drink. Then the water company changed to using the local river and people began to get sick. They complained that their water tasted and smelled bad, but nobody listened. Mari was just eight years old at this time and she wrote to ⁴ _____ president of her country. He read her letter ⁵ _____ visited the city. Soon after, he agreed to send $100 million to help. Since then, Mari has continued to ask for clean water across the whole country and also to fight for equal opportunities for everyone. ⁶ _____ own projects have raised more than $600,000 for kids.

2 What type of word is missing in each gap? Use the words in the box to describe them.

> article   auxiliary verb   linking word
> preposition   pronoun   verb

3 Read the text again. Write **one** word for each gap.

4 Work in pairs. Talk about the things you used to want to be or do when you were younger.

A: What did you use to want to be when you were younger?

B: I used to want to be a train driver. I used to run around our house with my toy trains. What about you?

WRITING

A LETTER

1 Read the advertisement. Are you interested in applying? Why? / Why not?

ⓦ Volunteer opportunities

Have you ever wanted to do a little more for your local area? We're looking for responsible young people who would like to work on <u>one</u> of the following projects in exchange for an unforgettable experience:

- Care for sick and injured wildlife in a rescue centre.
- Help at the annual coast clean-up. Free barbecue afterwards!
- Join the team at the community garden and learn to grow your own food!

Send Laura Diaz a letter saying which project you're interested in and why.

2 Read Katia's letter. Which project is she interested in? Would you accept her? Why? / Why not?

Dear Laura,

I am Katia and I am fifteen years old. Ever since I was little, I have always loved animals. As a small child, I used to make sure the birds in our neighbourhood had enough food during the winter. Growing up we did not have any pets, but I used to take our elderly neighbours' dogs for a walk.

The school holidays are approaching, and I would love to volunteer at an animal rescue centre during this time. Although I have never worked in an animal centre before, I understand that the work will be physically demanding. I am healthy and fit, and I believe I am completely reliable.

I hope that you will take my application into serious consideration for a place on this project.

Yours sincerely,

Katia Mills

3 Read the letter again. Which of these things does Katia include? Find them in the letter.

1 an appropriate opening
2 name and age
3 address
4 experience and skills
5 personal qualities
6 availability
7 a conclusion
8 an appropriate closing

4 Choose one of the other projects in the advertisement and write your own letter. Use Katia's letter to help you.

5 Read your letter again and revise your work. Use these questions to help you.

1 Have you included the important things from Exercise 3?
2 Have you used a range of tenses (present perfect, past simple and *used to*)?
3 Have you used some of the expressions from Katia's letter?
4 Can you see any problems with the language (spelling, grammar, etc.)?

6 Now work in pairs. Read each other's letters and give feedback. Use the questions in Exercise 5 to help you. Make a note of your partner's feedback and write a second draft of your letter.

7 Work in small groups. Read the group's letters and decide who should get a job as a volunteer.

8 📖 Read the model answer.

🛡 CHALLENGE ①②③④
Develop

1 In your group, compare and evaluate your list of ideas.
2 Decide which of the ideas you want to present to the class.
3 Decide how you will present the idea, for example on a poster or in a presentation.
4 Create a first draft.

LISTENING

A MONOLOGUE

1 Do you or anyone you know grow their own food?

2 Work in pairs and find some of these things in the photo.

> a leaf   seed   sprouts
> windowsill   window box

✓ **EXAM TASK** LISTENING PART 3

EXAM TIP

Read the questions carefully before you listen and think about what kind of word is missing in each gap.

3 Look at the exam question. How many words might be missing? What kinds of words might these be?

> For each question, write the correct answer in the gap. Write **one** or **two words** or a **number** or a **date** or a **time**.
>
> You will hear Tom Stubbs, an urban farmer, talking to a group of students about growing their own food.

Growing your own food

Vegetables won't grow without plenty of
(1) _____.
Tom Stubbs started planting lettuces
(2) _____ years ago.
You could add home-grown
(3) _____ to your salad, which you can grow from their seeds.
Tom uses garlic sprouts in his
(4) _____.
Instead of throwing away the green part of a
(5) _____, grow it in water.
You can learn about getting insects to visit your plants in our show on
(6) _____.

4 Work in pairs. What kind of word is missing in each of the gaps in the task in Exercise 3?

5 🔊 3.6 Listen and do the exam task. Then listen again and check your answers.

ORACY

Giving positive feedback

When you work with your partner, listen to their ideas and make positive comments like 'I agree! I'd like to try that too!' or 'That's a great idea!' This will encourage them both to say more and to feel good about themselves.

6 Choose the correct words to make the comments positive.

1 What a *cool / rubbish* idea!
2 You're absolutely *right / wrong* there!
3 That sounds *dull / interesting*.
4 You're full of *terrible / good* ideas!
5 You're an *awesome / awful* partner!
6 I really *disliked / enjoyed* working with you.

7 Work in pairs. Which of the suggestions for growing your own food would you like to try? Remember to listen to your partner's ideas and use some of the positive comments in Exercise 6.

🛡 CHALLENGE — ①②③④

Present

1 Make sure you have everything you need for your poster or presentation.
2 Check that everyone in your group knows what their role is.
3 Present your project to your class.
4 As a class, decide which of the ideas you'd like to carry out.

WRAP UP

Look back at the unit. Write down:

1. some new vocabulary you learned to talk about the natural world.
2. your main role in the challenge.
3. one use of the present perfect.
4. a sentence with *used to* in the affirmative and the negative.
5. something in the unit that you especially enjoyed.

⟡ Sustainability

1 Think of three activities to stay in touch with nature that can replace some of your screen time.

2 What benefits do these new activities bring to your daily life?

SELF-ASSESSMENT: UNIT 3

How confident do you feel about:

- finding the answers to multiple-choice questions in an article?
- answering an examiner's questions and giving personal information about yourself?
- writing a letter in response to an advertisement?
- listening for key words or phrases in a monologue?
- using the present perfect and past simple?
- using *used to* to talk about things that happened regularly?
- identifying and naming animals?
- using words to describe the landscape?
- presenting your project to the class and persuading them to take up your suggestions?

What was your favourite part of Unit 3? Tell your partner.

Ⓣ Creative Thinking Look at the self-assessment and think about the presentation of your project to the class. What changes could you make to make your point of view more convincing?

⟩⟩⟩ STRETCH! YOUR CHOICE

Now, choose an option.

Option 1:
Redesign the outdoor spaces in your school. Think about ideas which would benefit the students, the teachers and also the environment. Create a poster or presentation to present your ideas to the class.

Option 2:
Organise a class debate on the topic 'wild animals should not be kept in zoos'. Work in groups to create arguments for and against and hold the debate.

Option 3:
Design a small indoor garden for your classroom. Do some research on suitable plants, create the garden and look after it.

VOCABULARY REFERENCE

ANIMALS

1 Match the animals to the photos. How much do you know about each one?

bat   bee   deer   giraffe   goat   kangaroo   mosquito   owl   penguin   shark   wasp   zebra

LANDSCAPE

2 Match the landscape features to the photos. Which of the features can you see in your local area?

bay   canal   cave   cliff   coast   harbour   sand   shore   stream   valley

DIGITAL CLASSROOM

PRACTICE EXTRA UNIT 3

UNIT 4 HEALTHY AND HAPPY

LEARNING AIMS

- **Skills:** discuss and create texts about health
- **Grammar:** learn and practise modal verbs for advice, obligation and necessity
- **Vocabulary:** learn and practise words and phrases about health
- **Oracy:** speak confidently in a debate
- **Exam practice:** Reading Part 5, Speaking Part 3, Listening Part 4

ORACY

Having a debate
- using confident body language
- managing speaking time
- identifying weaker arguments

1 Look at the photo. Discuss the questions in small groups.

1. What are the people doing? Why?
2. How old do you think the different people in the picture are?
3. Is taking this kind of exercise equally important for all of them?

2 Watch the video. What three things are mentioned that can help you stay healthy?

▶ 01

3 In groups of three, look at the statements and select which one you'd like to discuss. Talk about it together and try to reach an agreement.

- Most teenagers don't have enough time for exercise.
- School and homework make it very hard for teenagers to get enough rest.
- It's hard to have a healthy lifestyle if you live in a big city.

4 Think about your group discussion in Exercise 3. Did you use any of the skills in the Oracy box? Which ones? Compare your answers.

Documentary

Grammar

Grammar

Oracy

VOCABULARY

BODY, HEALTH AND INJURY

1 🔲 ◁)) **4.1 Match the words to the numbers in the picture. Listen, check and repeat.**

ankle   bones   heel   hip   knee   shoulder
emergency   illness   injury   medicine
plaster   recovery

▶ Vocabulary reference page 46

2 ◁)) **4.2 Complete the page from a doctor's diary with the words from Exercise 1. Listen, check and repeat.**

What a day! It started with a(n) ¹ _____ : a student came in in an ambulance. He had broken two ² _____ . It was a sports ³ _____ .
He had hurt his ⁴ _____ , too, and couldn't move his arm. However, he will make a full ⁵ _____ . Some other people had fallen. Kids often fall and hurt their ⁶ _____ . It looks bad, but it isn't usually a big problem. It's worse when an old person falls and can't walk anymore because they've broken their ⁷ _____ . We had lots of people with flu – a typical ⁸ _____ at this time of year. ⁹ _____ can help a bit, but mostly the patients just have to rest and drink enough water. And then ... I was leaving the clinic when I fell down the steps and hurt my foot. I thought only my ¹⁰ _____ was hurt, but then I tried to stand up. No chance: I'd broken my ¹¹ _____ ! So now it's in ¹² _____ and I'm at home watching films. It sounds relaxing, but I'm bored!

3 **Complete the table. Use a dictionary or share what you know with classmates.**

Noun	Verb	Adjective
illness		3 _____
injury	1 _____	4 _____
medicine		5 _____
recovery	2 _____	6 _____

4 **Do you think these statements are true or false? Discuss in groups and then check the answers on page 124.**

1 The sport that causes the most injuries in the UK is rugby, and it is most common to injure the ankles or knees.

2 Your skin is thinnest on your shoulders and thickest on your heels.

3 The most common broken bone is the collar bone, near your shoulder. If you break it, it takes six to ten weeks to recover.

4 Taking deep breaths helps you feel calm, and will speed up your recovery if you are ill.

ORACY

Using confident body language

When you talk to a group, people are looking at you as well as listening. You need to look confident. Stand up and walk around slowly if you want to (but don't use classroom furniture to hold yourself up). Make eye contact with your audience.

5 **Work in groups of six students. Pick one of these statements, stand up and tell the others in your group whether you agree or disagree with it, and why.**

- Doctors and nurses should be the highest-paid professional people.
- Schools should offer one hour of sports every day.
- Extreme sports like bungee jumping should be banned.

6 **In your group, listen to the person who is speaking and give feedback using this checklist. Make a note of any extra comments you would like to make.**

	Yes / No
Did the speaker stand up?	
Did the speaker walk around?	
Did the speaker make eye contact?	
Did the speaker look confident?	

>> **STRETCH!** Talk to a person who has a job related to health or medicine. Write a short text about what they do on a typical workday. How many new vocabulary items on this page can you use?

READING

A SHORT TEXT

1 Work in pairs and discuss the questions. How much do you sleep? When do you sleep? Is it enough? Do you both have the same sleep patterns?

2 You are going to read an article called 'One night, two sleeps'. In pairs, talk about what you think it is about.

3 Read the first paragraph of the article and choose the correct word for the gap.

ONE NIGHT, TWO SLEEPS

🔊 4.3

We know that a good night's sleep is very important for our health. We want good beds and dark, quiet bedrooms. Experts say we should try to ¹ _____ asleep at regular times, and not too late.

1 A slip   B fall   C drop   D sink

☑ **EXAM TASK** READING PART 5

4 Read the rest of the article. For each question, choose the correct answer.

Going to sleep early, staying asleep and ² _____ up early is now considered the healthiest way to get enough rest. However, historians believe that our sleep patterns used to be very different. Before electric light was ³ _____, people went to bed much earlier than they do today. They slept for just a ⁴ _____ hours and then usually got up again, before going back to bed about two hours later for 'the second sleep'.

Problems with sleep are common nowadays, so should we ⁵ _____ to this old pattern? Well, it's not practical for people who go to school or work. We probably need to keep the sleep patterns we have now, even if they don't ⁶ _____ well for everyone.

5 Do you think 'One night, two sleeps' would be a good way for you to rest? Discuss in groups.

6 🎓 **Learning to Learn** Did you learn any new collocations or phrases in the article in Exercises 3 and 4? Write down three that you want to remember. Compare your three with a partner.

EXAM TIP

The verbs in Exercise 3 have similar meanings but only one forms a common collocation with *asleep*. Learning collocations and whole phrases will help you with this kind of exam task.

2	A starting	B going	C waking	D moving
3	A dreamed	B formed	C created	D invented
4	A few	B little	C many	D some
5	A recover	B repeat	C reduce	D return
6	A act	B work	C manage	D do

GRAMMAR
MODAL VERBS

1 Watch the grammar animation. Why is Hassan enjoying the trip to the museum more than Rebecca?

▶ 02

2 Look at the sentences from the grammar animation and complete the grammar rules.

1 We should make something like this in art class.
2 You must go to bed earlier.
3 You need to sleep more.
4 You've got to do more exercise.
5 We have to be quiet in the museum!

Modal verbs

1 The modal verb _____ tells us that something is a good idea.
2 The modal verbs _____, _____, _____ and _____ tell us that something is necessary or a rule.
3 The negative forms *don't have to* and _____ tell us that something is not necessary.
4 The negative form _____ tells us that something is not allowed or a very bad idea.

▶ Grammar reference and practice page 117

3 🖥 Go to the digital activities.

4 Complete the conversation with modal verbs. Sometimes more than one verb is possible.

Doctor: What's the problem?
Patient: I've injured my foot and it's getting worse. What [1]_____ I do?
Doctor: Well, you [2]_____ walk on it if it hurts. Let me have a look. Hmm, it's not too bad. Nothing is broken.
Patient: So can I play football tomorrow?
Doctor: No, I'm sorry but you [3]_____ do sports! You [4]_____ stay at home in bed, but you [5]_____ rest your foot.
Patient: How long [6]_____ I _____ rest my foot for?
Doctor: You [7]_____ be careful for two or three weeks. Come back and see me in two weeks.

5 🖥 PRONUNCIATION Go to the digital pronunciation activity.

6 Look at the problems. Work in pairs and give the people advice. Use modal verbs.

>>> STRETCH! Translate the sentences into your own language. Then write two sentences which explain the difference between *mustn't* and *don't have to*.

1 You mustn't go running every day.
2 You don't have to go running every day.

ORACY
Managing speaking time

If you want to say something important but you don't have much time, give a very short introduction and get to the main point quickly. Before you speak, make brief notes about your talk and estimate the time you need.

7 Work in pairs. Each student prepares a one-minute talk on one of the statements.

• Young people should do a lot of sports.
• Doing too much sport can be dangerous.

8 Student A, give your talk. Student B, listen and make sure your partner speaks for only one minute. What were your partner's main points? Make notes.

9 Compare your partner's notes with your notes from Exercise 7. Are the same main points there? Then swap roles.

HOW IS UNIT 4 SO FAR?

☆☆☆ I understand   ☆☆ I'm getting there   ☆ I don't understand

Dear Louise,

My parents don't understand how important it is to be healthy! I want to feel healthy and do well at school. Sport helps. I go jogging for an hour every day before breakfast. It's fun and it fills me with energy, but mum and dad think I should relax and stay in bed longer. They sit on the sofa and look at their mobile phones for hours, but that's bad for them! How can I convince them that being healthy is the most important thing in life?

Ben

Dear Ben,

It's great that you enjoy sport and that you want to be healthy. However, worrying is *un*healthy. Doctors in the USA say that one in three teenagers will experience health problems because they are anxious. It's normal to worry about some things in your life, but don't get anxious about things you can't change.

You go jogging every morning. I'm impressed! Just remember that it *is* possible to do too much sport, and your body needs downtime as well as exercise. You want to do well at school, and if jogging gives you energy and helps you to concentrate, that's great. However, if you feel that you *must* go jogging, it brings more stress into your life. Also, if you feel an ache in your knees or ankles, for example, then they need a break. Relaxing on the sofa can be enjoyable, too.

You can't change your parents' habits, so be patient with them. They need their relaxation. They clearly want you to be happy, so listen when they say you should relax more. They may be right!

Louise

READING

A PROBLEM PAGE

1 🔊 **4.4 Read and listen to Ben's problem. Is he worrying too much?**

2 🔊 **4.5 Read and listen to Louise's answer. Who does she agree with?**

3 **Answer the questions in your own words.**

1 How could Ben be hurting his health? Name two ways.
2 How could jogging help Ben at school?
3 How does a body sometimes warn someone that he/she is jogging too much?
4 Does Louise think that Ben should try to make his parents more active?
5 Why does Louise think Ben should listen to his parents?

4 🛡️ **Critical Thinking** **Users of this website can write comments after Louise's advice. Say what you think Ben should do and why you agree or disagree with Louise's advice.**

VOCABULARY

FEELING HEALTHY

1 🔊 **4.6 Look at the words. Which ones are nouns and which are adjectives? Listen, check and repeat.**

ache   anxious   downtime   energy
enjoyable   health check   impressed
operation   stress   stressful

2 🖥️ **Go to the digital activity and describe each photo and say how it makes you feel. Use the words from Exercise 1.**

▶ **Vocabulary reference page 46**

3 **Complete the conversation with the words from Exercise 1.**

Halida: Hi, Greg. How are you?

Greg: Great! I ran a half-marathon yesterday.

Halida: Wow, I'm ¹ _____! Was it ² _____? Or was it just hard?

Greg: Both. I really enjoyed it, but now I have a(n) ³ _____ in my foot. And I'm exhausted! I'm going to the doctor's tomorrow for a(n) ⁴ _____. I'm a little bit ⁵ _____ about it because my father had a(n) ⁶ _____ on his foot, and he wasn't allowed to run for months afterwards!

Halida: Don't worry. You're young and healthy. I know going to the doctor can be ⁷ _____, but your body probably just needs some ⁸ _____. I know you're always full of ⁹ _____, but it's important to slow down and relax a bit after something hard like a half-marathon.

Greg: I know you're right, but I really love running! It makes me forget about exams and ¹⁰ _____ at school. Sport makes me relaxed and happy.

GRAMMAR

OBLIGATION IN THE PRESENT AND PAST

1 Watch the grammar vlog. Why does Leo have so much fitness equipment?

▶ 03

2 Choose the correct modal verbs and then complete the grammar rules.

1 Yesterday, Leo *has to / had to* do a fitness test.
2 Now he says he *has to / had to* get fitter.
3 In the fitness test, the students *must / had to* do different kinds of exercise.
4 They *mustn't / didn't have to* swim or play football.
5 Leo *doesn't have to / didn't have to* do more sports, but he thinks it's a good idea.
6 He says, 'I *must / had to* remember to stretch before I run.'

> **Obligation in the present and past**
> 1 The modal verb _____ has no past form.
> 2 To talk about obligation in the past, we use _____ and _____.
>
> ▶ **Grammar reference and practice page 117**

3 🖥 Go to the digital activities.

♻ **4** Complete the text with the correct form of *must, have to* or *had to.*

My great-grandmother is 83. When she was young, they had different ideas about healthy living. She never liked meat, but she ¹ _____ eat it, as people believed it was essential for good health. Now we know that you ² _____ eat meat, but you ³ _____ make sure that you eat a wide variety of foods. You ⁴ _____ eat too much fast food. In the past, people didn't have all the fast food we have today, so they ⁵ _____ worry about that. They didn't know as much about hygiene back then. My great-grandmother ⁶ _____ wash her hands as often as we do now, and people certainly ⁷ _____ have a shower every day. If they wanted to have a bath, they ⁸ _____ heat the water first, which was expensive and took a long time.

👥 **MEDIATION WORKSHEET**

⟩⟩ STRETCH! Ask older people in your family about what they had to do in the past to be healthy. Then write a short text about it in English.

DIGITAL CLASSROOM ▶
PRACTICE EXTRA UNIT 4

SPEAKING

MAKING AND RESPONDING TO SUGGESTIONS

1 🔊 4.7 Listen to two students doing a Speaking Part 3 task. What do they have to do?

> **EXAM TIP**
>
> In Speaking Part 3, you will work with your partner. You have to give your own ideas, but also show that you can take part in a conversation. You can't speak all the time, so ask your partner questions and listen to their ideas.

2 🔊 4.7 Listen again. Which questions do you hear?

What do we want to eat?
How much space do you think we have in the kitchen?
How many dishes should we make?
What do you say?
What do you think this dish here is?
How many ingredients does it have?
How long does it take?

3 Questions that use 'do you think' are useful when you ask for another person's opinion or guess. Rewrite the questions with 'do you think'.

1 What does it cost?
What do you think it costs?
2 What ingredients do we need?
3 How long does it take?
4 How many plates do we need?
5 How much time do we have?
6 What kind of food do our classmates like?

✓ EXAM TASK SPEAKING PART 3

4 Work in pairs. Look at the picture on page 125. Your school is organising a 'Health Awareness Day' so students learn more about healthy food and activities. These are some activities your school could organise. Talk together about the different activities and say which would be the best.

WRITING

A DIARY ENTRY

1 Look at the photo. What is the girl drinking? Discuss in what ways this drink is healthier than fizzy drinks or fruit juices.

2 Look at Jasmine's list of goals and her diary entry. What did she achieve and what did she not achieve?

3 Look again at the list of goals and the diary entry and answer the questions.

   1 How many main points are there in Jasmine's list?

   2 How many main paragraphs are there in her diary entry?

   3 What is the function of the first, short paragraph?

4 Work in pairs and think of things you could do to be healthy this weekend. Help each other make a checklist with three main points.

5 Imagine it is Monday morning. Do you think you have achieved your goals? Write a diary entry like Jasmine's.

6 Read your diary entry again and revise your work. Use these questions to help you.

   1 Have you started with a short introduction?

   2 Have you written about three main points?

   4 Have you written three main paragraphs?

   5 Can you see any problems with the language (spelling, grammar, etc.)?

7 Now work in pairs. Read each other's diary entries and give feedback. Use the questions in Exercise 6 to help you. Make a note of your partner's feedback and write a second draft.

8 Read the model answer.

>>> STRETCH! Take your list of goals home and try to achieve your goals this weekend. On Monday, write a diary entry about what you achieved.

GOALS THIS WEEKEND:

* 8 hours of sleep each night
* Saturday: go to bed before 10.30 pm
* Sunday: go to bed before 9.30 pm
  * walk 10,000 steps each day
  * drink 1.5 litres of water

Diary

Saturday 15.05 and Sunday 16.05

My goals this weekend were to get enough sleep, walk enough steps and drink enough water.

I got more than eight hours' sleep on Saturday night because I stayed in bed late on Sunday morning. I didn't go to bed early on Saturday night, but I went to bed at nine o'clock on Sunday, so I got enough sleep and wasn't tired on Monday morning.

I used my fitness watch to count my steps. On Saturday I met my friends and we went to a lot of different places on foot. I walked over 12,000 steps. On Sunday I walked over 11,000 steps. That wasn't as many as on Saturday, but I was out in the forest with my parents, so that's good.

I forgot to count how much I drank! I don't think it was enough. I can enter each drink on my fitness watch, but I always forget. My plan for next week is to hang a drinks checklist in the kitchen. When I have a drink, I only have to put a tick on the list. That's easy.

LISTENING

AN INTERVIEW

1 Have you ever had a drink like in the photo when you were sick?

2 You will hear an interview with a doctor. First, look at this question. Do any of the answers look as if they *couldn't* be right?

   1 Dr Walsh says staying inside
     A is the best way to stay healthy in winter.
     B will not stop you from catching a cold.
     C can make you lazy and unfit.

> ### EXAM TIP
>
> Many of the answers in Part 4 sound like they might be right, so you need to listen carefully to understand exactly what the interviewee says. You can't usually use your world knowledge to answer the questions.

3 🔊 **4.8 Listen to the first part of the interview and choose the correct answer in Exercise 2. Check your answer with a partner.**

> ### ✓ EXAM TASK   LISTENING PART 4
>
> **4** 🔊 **4.9 Listen to the rest of the interview. For each question 2–6, choose the correct answer.**
>
>   2 What advice does Dr Walsh give about going out in cold weather?
>   **A** It's a good idea to cover your head.
>   **B** You should protect your nose and throat.
>   **C** It's best to go back to a warm room quickly.
>   3 What does Dr Walsh think about swimming in very cold water?
>   **A** Nobody should do it.
>   **B** It's a good way to feel strong.
>   **C** It's not safe for everyone.
>   4 Dr Walsh says that garlic
>   **A** is better than medicine when you have a cold.
>   **B** can't stop you from catching a cold.
>   **C** is generally good for your health.
>   5 Dr Walsh says warm drinks are good when you've got a cold because
>   **A** drinking enough is important.
>   **B** they'll make your cold go away sooner.
>   **C** they contain healthy ingredients.
>   6 What positive information does Dr Walsh give the listeners?
>   **A** We can stay home and relax when we're sick.
>   **B** A cold will always go away in the end.
>   **C** In the future, we won't catch colds.

> ### ORACY
> #### Identifying weaker arguments
>
> It's important to have good arguments in a debate, but you also need to find weaknesses in the other side's arguments. Listen very carefully when they speak and remember anything you think is not quite right. You can focus on that when it's your turn to speak again.

5 🔊 **4.10 Listen to a student talking about another student's argument in a debate and answer the questions.**

   1 What was the debate about?
     A The best ways for young people to stay fit.
     B The best sports for young people to do.
   2 How does the speaker show us that he's going to disagree with what Kim said?

6 Look at these two arguments and pick one that you think has a weakness. Write what you would say in a debate to identify that weakness.

> Modern medicine is wonderful and can help with all kinds of problems. Medicine can now save people who have very serious illnesses, so it can certainly save us when we've got a cold. We just need to go to the pharmacy, get the right medicine and our cold will go away in a few hours.

> Team sports played outside are very good for your health. You get really good exercise, breathe fresh air and practise thinking and reacting fast, too. All schools should offer these sports. They shouldn't offer sports like swimming or gymnastics, which don't have the same benefits.

ORACY

HAVING A DEBATE

- using confident body language
- managing speaking time
- identifying weaker arguments

1 Work in groups. You are going to watch some students having a 'hat debate'. Do you know what a hat debate is? Tell your group or guess together what it might be.

2 Watch some students planning a hat debate and answer the questions.

1 Were you right about what a hat debate is?
2 What do the students find difficult now?
3 What do they think could be difficult about the debate?

3 ▶ 05 Now watch two students, Daria and Kamal, having the debate. Answer the questions.

1 Which student had the most confident body language?
2 Which student managed his/her time best?
3 What weakness did the second student find in the first student's argument?

4 ▶ 06 Watch the group discussing the debate and answer the questions.

1 Who won the debate?
2 Why is the result so surprising for Kamal?
3 What aspect of her performance does Daria think should have been better?

5 Prepare to have a hat debate. Follow these steps.

- Write debate topics (e.g., health, sport, food and drink, etc.) on slips of paper and put them in a hat. Include your own ideas as well.
- A pair of students will pick a topic from the hat and start. The teacher decides which student argues for and which against the motion.
- The two students have five minutes to prepare their arguments.

6 Hold the debate. Each student has a few one-minute turns to speak. The teacher stops the debate, and the other students vote for a winner.

7 Use this checklist to decide who to vote for.

	Did Student A…	How well did he/she do it?	Did Student B …	How well did he/she do it?
use confident body language?	✓ ✗	☹ ☺	✓ ✗	☹ ☺
manage the speaking time?	✓ ✗	☹ ☺	✓ ✗	☹ ☺
identify weaker arguments?	✓ ✗	☹ ☺	✓ ✗	☹ ☺

SELF-ASSESSMENT: UNIT 4

How confident do you feel about:

- reading about and responding to people who want advice? ☹ ☹ 😐 ☺
- identifying opinions and information in a longer interview? ☹ ☹ 😐 ☺
- discussing options with a partner? ☹ ☹ 😐 ☺
- writing a diary entry about your goals? ☹ ☹ 😐 ☺
- using modal verbs to make suggestions or talk about necessity? ☹ ☹ 😐 ☺
- using modal verbs for necessity and obligation in the past? ☹ ☹ 😐 ☺
- using words and phrases about health? ☹ ☹ 😐 ☺
- holding a debate? ☹ ☹ 😐 ☺

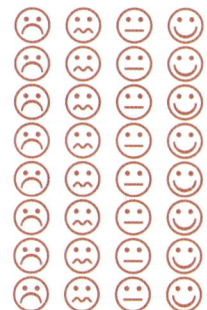

What was your favourite part of Unit 4? Tell your partner.

DIGITAL CLASSROOM
PERSONALISED LEARNING

VOCABULARY REFERENCE

BODY, HEALTH AND INJURY

1 Match the words to the numbers in the picture.

ankle · bones · heel · hip · knee · shoulder · emergency · injury · illness · medicine · plaster · recovery

DIGITAL CLASSROOM
PRACTICE EXTRA UNIT 4

FEELING HEALTHY

2 Describe each photo and say how it makes you feel. Use the words in the table.

Nouns						Adjectives			
ache	downtime	energy	health check	operation	stress	anxious	enjoyable	impressed	stressful

UNIT 5 TOO MUCH TRAVEL?

LEARNING AIMS

- **Skills:** discuss and create texts about travel
- **Grammar:** review and practise different future forms: *be going to*, present continuous and present simple
- **Vocabulary:** learn and practise words and phrases for travel and places
- **Collaboration:** work together to plan an environmentally friendly holiday
- **Exam practice:** Reading Part 3, Speaking Part 4, Writing Part 1 (email)

THE CHALLENGE

Travel is exciting but can be very bad for our planet. You will:

- **Stage 1 Think:** find out more about travel and the environment.
- **Stage 2 Prepare:** focus on one type of holiday which doesn't affect our planet as much.
- **Stage 3 Develop:** share information and plan a presentation.
- **Stage 4 Present:** present an environmentally friendly holiday.

1 **Look at the photo. Discuss the questions in small groups.**

1 Is this the beginning, middle or end of a journey? How do you know?
2 Would you like to be on the plane? Why? / Why not?
3 Is this a peaceful picture? How does it make you feel?

2 **Watch the video. Name one exciting thing that most young people look forward to and one important thing that they worry about.**

▶ 01

CHALLENGE ①─②─③─④

Think

Discuss the questions with a partner and make notes.

1 How can travel and holidays damage our planet? Make a list of situations.
2 Are some types of travel or holiday worse than others?
3 What types of holiday could be less damaging? Make a list.

Documentary

Grammar

Speaking

Grammar

VOCABULARY

TRAVEL

1 📱 🔊 **5.1 Go to the digital activity and match the words to the photos. Listen, check and repeat.**

airline   cabin   cruise ship   delay   fare
ferry   fuel   landing   reservation   route
take-off   vehicles

▶ Vocabulary reference page 56

2 **Complete the conversation with the correct form of words from Exercise 1.**

Mother: Let's go on a cruise for our summer holiday this year.

Son: Mum, no! It's boring staying on a ship all the time and anyway, big ¹ _____ are bad for the environment.

Mother: But you don't have to stay on the ship. You can get off and look around the local city. Plus you can take a really interesting ² _____ from one exciting city to the next. OK, what do you want to do?

Son: Let's just fly to a city near the sea and relax. There are ³ _____ that offer very low ⁴ _____, aren't there? We can make a ⁵ _____ at a hotel near the beach, and then you can visit the city, and dad and I can do water sports.

Mother: Wait, you're worried about the environment, but you want to fly? Now *that's* bad for the planet!

Son: OK, I have a better idea. We drive to the coast, take the car on the ⁶ _____ to an island and stay there.

Mother: That's a little bit better but the car burns ⁷ _____, too, and that's not good for the environment. All ⁸ _____ are damaging, except our bicycles. Oh, that gives me an idea!

Son: Oh no, Mum, not a cycling tour! I want to hang out with other kids on the beach!

3 **What are the people talking about? Match the words to the sentences (1–4).**   👥 **MEDIATION WORKSHEET**

the cabin   delays   take-off   landing

1 I love the moment when the plane leaves the ground.

2 Not me! I'm much happier when the plane comes back to earth.

3 There's never enough space in the part where the passengers sit.

4 It's really annoying when the plane doesn't leave on time.

4 **Work in pairs and discuss the questions.**

1 Do you like to travel by plane or think you would like it? Why? / Why not?

2 What vehicle do you use the most in everyday life? What are the advantages and disadvantages of that kind of transport?

5 🛡 **Critical Thinking** **Think back to the video and discuss the questions.**

1 Why does tourism sometimes cause problems with water?

2 Why is Barcelona extremely crowded on some days?

3 Do you think a place can have too many tourists?

ORACY

Getting everyone's opinions

People in a group will have different experiences. Make sure to include everyone in a discussion so that you don't miss important information and opinions.

6 🔊 **5.2 Listen to three young people, Owen, Lily and Max, talking about tourism in their town and answer the questions.**

1 Who speaks the most: Owen, Lily or Max?

2 Who speaks the least?

3 Why could Max's opinion be especially important in this discussion?

4 How does Lily improve the situation in the end?

>>> STRETCH! **Why do some places have a lot of tourists? Make a list of things that can make a place good for holidays.**

🛡 CHALLENGE ①②③④

Prepare

1 Form groups of three or four people.

2 Look at your list of more environmentally friendly holidays.

3 Decide what type of holiday you want to plan.

4 Talk about where you could find information. You'll need to know more about the holiday activities, where they could take place and why the holiday is both fun and sustainable.

5 Start your research.

READING

AN ONLINE ARTICLE

1 Becca and Bryn have a blog about holidays and trips away. What are they planning? Skim the blog post.

EXAM TIP

Skimming the text before you start answering the questions is a good idea in Part 3. It will be easier when you know what the whole text is about.

☑ EXAM TASK   READING PART 3

Becca and Bryn – the travelling twins   ✕   +

TREEHOUSE HOLIDAY

🔊 5.3

It's holiday time and our parents said Becca and I can choose what kind of holiday we want this year. Like so many other teenagers, we want to take care of our planet, and that matters on holiday, too. We've decided our aim is to plan the most environmentally friendly holiday possible.

We don't want to use a car or a plane, so we've found a place that sounds great, not far from our home. We're going to get there by train, and bring our bikes, and we're going to stay in a treehouse. You can get luxury treehouses nowadays, with heating, a bath, a TV … but that's not the type of place we're going to stay in. Our treehouse has beds, and that's all. It's a bit like camping, but in trees. There's one shared bathroom for ten treehouses, with warm water from solar* energy, and there are places to cook outside.

We certainly won't waste energy with our phones because there's no internet anywhere in the treehouse park. And do you know how much electricity one simple internet search uses? Well, nobody can say exactly but it's more than you think. We'll have no wi-fi and no phone reception in the forest. So that's saving energy, too.

But will it be a fun holiday for teens? We think so! We're going to cycle to a lake every day for swimming and water sports (no noisy boats or jet skis, though!). We're going to cook over an open fire, which is something we always enjoy. I'm going to read a lot and Becca's going to play her guitar. People always come and talk to us when they hear her music, so I think we'll meet other people our age and really enjoy the time together. Let's see! We're leaving tomorrow and we'll write a post about it for you when we come back, two weeks from now.

*created by the sun

2 Read the first paragraph of the blog post carefully and choose the correct answer. What phrase in the first paragraph shows you which answer is right?

1   What is most important to Becca and Bryn when choosing their next holiday?
   A   There is a big choice of things to do.
   B   They can travel around the world.
   C   It does not damage the world too much.
   D   People at their destination are nice to them.

3 Read the rest of the blog post carefully. For questions 2–5, choose the correct answer.

2   The treehouse they will stay in
   A   is very warm and comfortable.
   B   has a bathroom and kitchen in it.
   C   looks like a tent.
   D   is very simple accommodation.

3   Why will it be hard to use a phone on the holiday?
   A   No phones are allowed in the treehouse park.
   B   They will have to go outdoors to phone people.
   C   They won't be able to make calls or go online.
   D   They won't have energy to charge the phones.

4   They think the holiday will be good because
   A   they will do fun things with other teenagers.
   B   there will be a lot of music in the treehouse park.
   C   they can go on a fast motorboat every day.
   D   they will learn a new way of cooking.

5   What might a review of the treehouse park say?
   A   An amazing holiday park for people who want to try a wide variety of adventure sports.
   B   A holiday in nature that shows how much fun you can have without technology that damages the environment.
   C   A holiday that offers exciting activities during the day and entertainment options like films and music at night.
   D   A quiet, beautiful place for old and young visitors who want some relaxing time alone.

GRAMMAR

BE GOING TO AND THE PRESENT CONTINUOUS FOR FUTURE ARRANGEMENTS

1 **Watch the grammar vlog. Why is Alex excited?**
▶ 02

2 Look at the sentences and complete the grammar rules with *be going to* or *the present continuous*.

> **be going to and the present continuous for future arrangements**
>
> *Dad is driving me to the bus at seven.*
> *The hostel is going to make us packed lunches.*
>
> 1 We use _____ to talk about things someone plans to do in the future.
> 2 We use _____ to talk about arrangements someone has made for a fixed time in the future.
>
> ▶ Grammar reference and practice page 118

3 🖳 Go to the digital activities.

4 🖳 (PRONUNCIATION) Go to the digital pronunciation activity.

5 Read the timetable for one day of the school trip to Edinburgh and write answers to the questions.

1 When is the class having breakfast on Friday?
2 What are they going to do after breakfast?
3 When are they visiting Edinburgh Castle?
4 Where are they having lunch?
5 What is Alex going to do in the afternoon?
6 What time are they going to the theatre?

SPEAKING

DISCUSSING LIKES, DISLIKES, EXPERIENCES, OPINIONS AND HABITS

1 **Watch two candidates answering questions in Speaking Part 4. Who is better? Why?**
▶ 03

2 ▶ 03 Watch the video again and explain in your own words why:

1 Antonio thinks a city trip is educational.
2 Lara thinks a city trip is fun.
3 Antonio thinks people should see the capital city of their country.
4 Lara thinks it's best to visit a city with friends.

☑ EXAM TASK SPEAKING PART 4

EXAM TIP

In Part 4 of the Speaking exam, the examiner will ask about your opinions. Say what you think and then say why this is your opinion. Thinking about *why* helps you to give fuller answers.

3 Look at the examiner's questions and candidate's answers. Which answers do you agree with? Pick two. Say the sentence and then add two more sentences explaining your opinion.

Examiner: Do you think all students should go on school trips?
A: Yes, everyone should go on school trips.
B: I think school trips should only be for students who want to go on them.
Examiner: Is travelling a good way to learn about the world?
A: Yes! You learn more in a week of travelling than in a month at school.
B: No. Travel and holidays are for relaxing and not for learning.

EDINBURGH TRIP – Friday Alex

08.00	breakfast in hostel
09.00	walk through town centre
10.30	visit Edinburgh Castle
13.30	picnic lunch, Princes Street Gardens

15.00	free time in the park or cèilidh 😃
18.00	dinner (restaurant near hostel)
19.30	theatre

LISTENING

AN INTERVIEW

1 Look at the photo. The mother and daughter are 'digital nomads' – they travel around the world and do their work and schooling via the internet wherever they are. Would you like that lifestyle? Discuss in pairs.

2 🔊 **5.4** Listen to an interview with Katrin, a girl from a digital **nomad family**, and answer the questions.

   1   Is Katrin happy about being a digital nomad?

   2   How much travelling does she want to do when she is an adult?

3 🔊 **5.4** Listen again. Correct the mistakes in the sentences.

   1   Now Katrin and her family are living on a boat in Venice.

   2   She enjoys going to different embassies around the world.

   3   She has had good experiences at airports.

   4   Living in New York was the best because it was relaxing.

   5   Katrin and her parents say Brighton is their home.

   6   Next year, they are moving to Costa Rica.

4 🛡 **Critical Thinking** Has your opinion about being a digital nomad changed after listening to Katrin? In groups, make lists of the good things and the bad things about the way Katrin lives. Then try to agree on whether it is a good way to live.

HOW IS UNIT 5 SO FAR?

☆☆☆ I understand   ☆☆ I'm getting there   ☆ I don't understand

---

VOCABULARY

PLACES

1 📷 🔊 **5.5** Go to the digital activity and match the words to the photos. Listen, check and repeat.

> continent   customs   crossroads
> embassy   gate   immigration
> rainforest   region   subway   tunnel

▶ **Vocabulary reference page 56**

2 Complete the conversation with words from Exercise 1.

> **Oscar:** My dream is to live in a really huge city. Maybe I'll live in Asia. I think that's the
> ¹ _____ with the most exciting cities. My dream city has a good ² _____ system, so that you don't have to drive a car. And for people who need their cars, there's a ³ _____ under the city. So it's a busy city, but not noisy and polluted.

> **Lucy:** My dream is to live in a(n) ⁴ _____ of the world where there are not many people. I want to live in a beautiful green ⁵ _____. Yes, really! There are no busy streets and dangerous ⁶ _____. There are only rivers, where people travel by boat. It's a place where people feel free.

3 Would you most like to live in the city or the countryside? Tell a partner about the place where your dream home would be.

4 Match the words to the definitions.

> customs   embassy   gate   immigration

   1   You go there to get a visa for a country you want to visit.

   2   This is where you leave the airport and board the plane.

   3   They check your passport and maybe your visa here.

   4   Before you leave the airport, you might have to open your bags here.

⟫⟫ STRETCH! In New York, they have a *subway*. In British English, this is called the *underground* (or in London, the *tube*). Think of more words that are different in American and British English. Make a list.

GRAMMAR

PRESENT SIMPLE FOR THE FUTURE

1 Watch the grammar animation. What does Sophie want to do?

▶ 04

2 Look at the examples from the grammar animation and complete the grammar rule with the correct words.

> **Present simple for the future**
> *When do they play? His band start at eight.*
> We can use the _____ as the 'timetable future'.
> We use it most often to talk about events that are fixed in timetables, or to say when something happening in the future begins or ends.
>
> ▶ Grammar reference and practice page 118

3 🔲 Go to the digital activities.

4 Complete the conversation with the present simple or present continuous form of the verbs in brackets.

A: I'm going to visit my cousin in Berlin next weekend. It'll be fun, I hope.

B: Great. How [1] _____ you _____ (get) there?

A: I [2] _____ (fly) of course. I've never flown before and I'm nervous. Luckily, my brother [3] _____ (come) with me.

B: When [4] _____ the flight _____ (leave)?

A: Let's see, I have the ticket here. It [5] _____ (depart) at 9.45. Check-in [6] _____ (open) three hours before that.

B: Do we really have to be there three hours earlier?

A: Well, [7] _____ you _____ (check in) a bag?

B: No, we [8] _____ just _____ (take) hand luggage. We [9] _____ only _____ (stay) for a weekend.

A: Then maybe you don't have to be there three hours before the flight. But two hours at least!

B: OK. We want to catch a train that [10] _____ (arrive) at the airport at 7.15. That's fine, isn't it?

A: Probably, but don't miss that train! Any later train will be too late.

5 Imagine you are going away next weekend. Make some notes about these points.

- Where?
- How? (train, flight …)
- Who with?
- some plans when you are there
- departure time
- arrival time

6 Work in pairs and ask and answer questions about your travel plans from Exercise 5. Use the present simple and present continuous, or other future forms if they fit.

> **DIGITAL CLASSROOM**
> PRACTICE EXTRA UNIT 5

ORACY

Giving positive feedback

Other people will enjoy talking to you if you give positive feedback. You don't have to agree with what they say, but tell them things you like about what they've said. Use phrases like *That sounds great! / … is a good idea. / That's really interesting.*

7 Tell your partner what you think of his/her travel plans. Give some positive feedback! Use some phrases from the oracy tip, and some of your own.

>>> STRETCH! You have learned several future forms. Look online for other future tenses. What can you find? What are they used for? Compare your answers with a partner.

CHALLENGE ①②③④

Develop

1 Decide how you will present what you have learned by reading, for example, on a poster or through a presentation.

2 Make a list of headings you can use, e.g. *Type of holiday / Where? / Advantages*.

3 Choose the information to put under each heading.

4 Create a first draft, for example of a poster or of notes for a presentation.

WRITING

AN EMAIL

1 Look at the photos and say what the people are learning to do. Would you like to try any of these activities on a school trip?

2 Read the two emails. Does Maria answer all of Christoph's questions?

< Inbox — 2 Messages — ∧ ∨

Dear Maria,

We're having a school trip to your fantastic town!

We can give our teachers ideas about what cool activity we want to do there. You do a lot of exciting things in your free time. What's the best thing to do? Where can we do it?

Is there any special food that we can eat in your town? Where's the best place to eat it? Please tell me your ideas!

Christoph

< Inbox — 1 Message — ∧ ∨

Dear Christoph,

Wow, that's great news!

I think you should get fish and chips and eat it on the beach. That's more fun than going to an expensive restaurant, and the fish is really fresh and good.

The Adventure Centre in Lakeside Park is a great place to go. I go climbing there, which is a lot of fun. If you don't like climbing, you can learn canoeing or sailing on the lake. There's something for everyone.

Do you like Indian food? We've got restaurants with food from all over the world, but I like the Indian restaurants the best.

Have a fantastic time!

Maria

---

3 Maria gives a lot of information but her answer is not well organised. Look at the four questions and write them in the order she answers them. What is the problem?

What's the best thing to do?

Where can we do it?

Is there any special food that we can eat in your town?

Where's the best place to eat it?

☑ **EXAM TASK** WRITING PART 1

EXAM TIP

The email in the task makes it easy for you to organise your answer. Use the four notes in the order in which they are given.

4 Read this email from your cousin. Work in pairs and think about what your 'exciting activity' could be. Think of things you really do and things you would like to do, even if you can't!

< Inbox — 4 Messages — ∧ ∨

Hi!

Have you seen my new travel blog? I write about people I know in different places and what they do there. ——— **sounds exciting**

I want to write about you and your town. Mum says you do an exciting activity there but she can't remember what! What is it? ——— **tell Marcus**

Where do you do it? ——— **say where**

Is it something tourists could do? If it is, I want to write about it! ——— **explain why / why not**

Thanks for your help,

Marcus

5 Write your email to Marcus using all the notes.

6 Read your email again and revise it. Use these questions to help you.

1 Have you started with a suitable expression (*Dear Marcus / Hi Marcus*, etc.)?

2 Have you included all four points in the notes?

3 Have you given the information in a logical order?

4 Have you finished with a friendly phrase (*See you soon / All the best*, etc.)?

7 Now work in pairs. Read each other's emails and give feedback. Use the questions in Exercise 6 to help you. Make a note of your partner's feedback and write a second draft of your email.

8 🔊 Read the model answer.

LISTENING

AN INTERVIEW

1 Look at the photos. Which activities do you think are expensive and which are cheap? Discuss in groups.

2 🔊 5.6 You will hear an interview with a young man called Matti who is talking about saving money when you go on a trip. Which of the things do you think will be recommended as inexpensive options? Listen and check.

- picnics
- parks
- campsites
- fast food
- youth hostels
- tourist shops

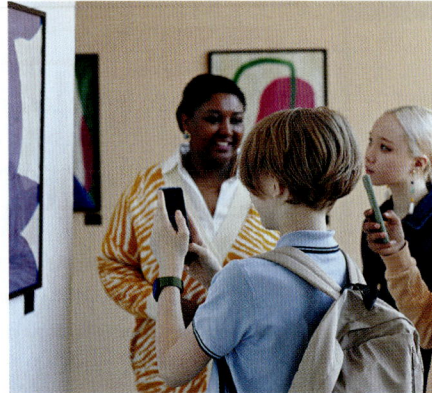

3 🔊 5.6 Listen again and answer the questions in your own words.

1 Does Matti think a beach holiday can be a cheap option?
2 What could go wrong if you spend all day on a beach?
3 Why might you spend less money in cities with warm weather?
4 What might be free on some days of the week?
5 What might be cheaper on some days of the week?
6 Where could you find useful tips about a place?
7 Where can you go for help after you've arrived in a new place?
8 Why can it be expensive if you don't pack the right things?

4 What is the best summary of Matti's main message?

A You can best save money by reading a good travel blog.
B It is most important to stay away from big, expensive cities.
C Good planning is the key to saving money on a trip away.

5 How can people have fun in your town without spending money? Work in pairs and make a list of tips you would give a visitor.

ORACY

Offering examples

If you want to give someone advice, it's useful to give clear examples of how to follow it. For example, 'stay safe on holiday' is good advice. It's even better to give examples, such as 'tell people where you are going' or 'plan how to go places so that you don't get lost'.

6 🔊 5.7 Listen to part of the interview with Matti. He says you should find out when things are cheapest in a city. What two examples does he give to show what he means?

7 Look at these pieces of holiday advice for teens. Choose one that you think is important, read it out and then give one or two examples to show what you mean.

1 Be careful with your money on holiday.
2 Make sure you have the right clothes.
3 Stay in contact with your family.

CHALLENGE 1 2 3 4

Present

1 Check that the information is clear in your first draft.
2 Practise explaining your poster / making your presentation.
3 Create a second draft.
4 Present your holiday to your classmates.

WRAP UP

Look back at the unit. Write down:

① some new vocabulary you learned to talk about travel.

② your main role in the challenge.

③ an example of the present continuous for talking about the future.

④ an example of the present simple for talking about the future.

⑤ something in the unit that you especially enjoyed.

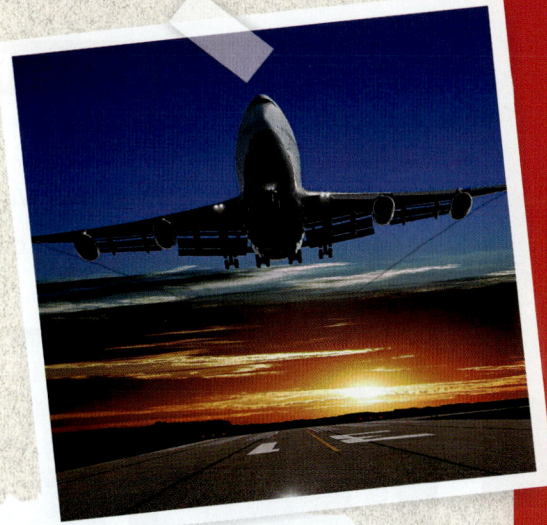

⟳ Sustainability

1 What is your favourite holiday? Why is it special for you?

2 Think of one activity that could make your favourite holiday sustainable. Tell a partner.

SELF-ASSESSMENT: UNIT 5

How confident do you feel about:

- skimming an article for general meaning?
- reading carefully to answer questions about detail?
- sharing and explaining your opinions with a partner?
- writing a well-organised email to a friend?
- listening for useful information in an interview?
- using different future forms for plans and predictions?
- using vocabulary for travel and places?
- presenting environmentally friendly ways to have a holiday?

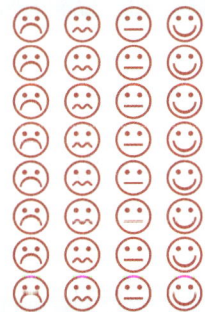

What was your favourite part of Unit 5? Tell your partner.

Learning to Learn Make a note of the areas in the self-assessment you need more help with. Do some extra practice and complete the self-assessment again in two weeks.

⟫ STRETCH! YOUR CHOICE

Now, choose an option.

Option 1:
Make a video about a place or sight in your town which could be interesting for tourists. If you can, go there and show the place in your video.

Option 2:
Find out more about one type of transport, e.g. flying or driving a car, and how it affects the environment. Make a fact file about it and show it to your classmates.

Option 3:
Create a class holiday blog where students can tell travel stories, post photos and recommend places to go (far away or closer to home). Keep it updated with real holiday ideas.

VOCABULARY REFERENCE

TRAVEL

1 Match the words to the photos. Which of these things are negative?

airline   cabin   cruise ship   delay   fare   ferry   fuel
landing   reservation   route   take-off   vehicles

PLACES

2 Match the words to the photos.

continent   customs   crossroads   embassy   gate   immigration
rainforest   region   subway   tunnel

DIGITAL CLASSROOM
PRACTICE EXTRA UNIT 5

UNIT 6 HOME AND AWAY

LEARNING AIMS

Skills: discuss and create texts about places to live

Grammar: learn and practise *can* for ability, present and past passive, causative *have/get*

Vocabulary: learn and practise words and phrases for house and home and household objects

Oracy: structure a guided tour

Exam practice: Reading Part 2, Speaking Part 1, Listening Part 1

ORACY

Giving a talk

- sequencing ideas for structure
- using appropriate gestures and body language
- engaging the audience

1 Look at the photo. Discuss the questions in small groups.

1 What can you see? Who do you think lives there?

2 Why do you think we like looking around other people's houses?

3 Whose house would you most like to look around? Why?

2 Watch the video. What tip do you think is the most useful? Why?

3 Work in small groups. Each person prepares a short tour of their perfect house. Listen carefully to each tour and decide which house you would most like to visit.

4 Think about the tours in Exercise 3. Did you use any of the skills in the Oracy box? Which ones? Compare your answers.

Documentary

Grammar

Grammar

Oracy

HOUSE AND HOME

1 🖼️ 🔊 **6.1 Go to the digital activity and find these things in the pictures. Then listen to all the words and repeat.**

basin   bedside table   blind

chest of drawers   curtain   duvet

fan   ground/first/second floor

pipe   upstairs/downstairs

▶ **Vocabulary reference page 66**

2 **Complete the advertisement with the correct form of some of the words in Exercise 1.**

THE HAINES SHOE HOUSE

Come and stay in a shoe!

Enjoy a special stay in the shoe house! The 'Shoe Wizard', Mahlon Haines, built his shoe house in 1948 to advertise his shoe shops. He built the Haines Shoe House on five
1 _____ as a guesthouse and up to six of you can now rent it!

The house has got lots of beautiful windows but there aren't any [2] _____ or [3] _____ because you wouldn't want to cover the coloured glass, would you? The kitchen has got plenty of cupboards and a large sink. [4] _____, on different levels, there are 3 bedrooms and 2 ½ bathrooms. There's a choice of baths and showers and of course, a(n) [5] _____ for washing your hands. In the bedrooms, there's a(n) [6] _____ on the bed, a(n) [7] _____ next to it and there's also plenty of space to put your clothes in the [8] _____.

3 **Work in pairs and think about your own perfect house. Which of the things in Exercise 1 has it got?**

4 **Read the house tour and match the paragraphs to the places.**

room   garage   garden   kitchen   my town

Welcome to my city!

1 This area used to be farms for many years. Then, in 1892, a weekly market started here and more people came. _____, in 1982, it became the most important trade centre in the region! My house has been here for more than fifty years!

2 _____ our tour out here. This is where my family have barbecues on weekends.

3 This room looks boring, but listen. _____ 2005, my mom secretly built a bicycle here for my birthday!

4 _____, we have my favourite room. Here I'm learning to cook simple but healthy meals.

5 _____, we have my room. It's small but it's very functional.

ORACY

Sequencing ideas for structure

When we're talking about a place, we can use sequencing words like *let's start with*, *next* and *ninety years later* to organise our ideas and give them a structure. This will create a clear beginning, middle and end.

5 **Read the tour again and complete the sentences with the sequencers.**

back in   last but not least
let's begin   next   ninety years later

6 **Work in pairs and find out about a famous place in your area. Prepare a short tour using the sequencers in Exercise 5. Don't include the name of the place.**

7 **Work in groups. Take turns to give your tour and guess the place. Was it easy to follow the tour?**

SHORT TEXTS

1 Read what the people are looking for and <u>underline</u> the most important things.

1		Lia and her family would like to get out and enjoy nature for a long weekend. Lia uses a wheelchair and the accommodation needs to be easy to get to by public transport.
2		Morgan wants to spend a week with his dad and sister. They'd all rather be on the coast as they're keen swimmers. They'll need somewhere to leave their bikes though.
3		Sara's family have got tickets for a play in the city next weekend but will need somewhere to stay, preferably within walking distance of the theatre. They fancy eating out and will travel by car.
4		Ben and his mum would like to celebrate her 50th birthday next Tuesday by staying overnight in the countryside. They don't want to cook and they want to go hiking.
5		Manish and his cousins want a reasonable apartment for six with reliable internet for gaming. They would love to be able to see the city from the flat but they plan to go sightseeing, too.

✓ EXAM TASK READING PART 2

2 Read the descriptions of eight accommodation options. Decide which option (A–H) would be most suitable for the people in Exercise 1 (1–5). Three options are not needed.

EXAM TIP

To match the people with their most suitable option, look for words in the descriptions (1–5) which have a similar meaning to the words in the options (A–H). You will not find the same words, but you will find words/phrases that mean the same thing.

MEDIATION WORKSHEET

A Jill's palace

This gorgeous sixth-floor flat with incredible views over the city is conveniently located in the centre. It's fully wheelchair friendly. You can get to the shopping centre, restaurants and the theatre on foot. No extra charge for the accommodation at weekends or for parking, but no wi-fi.

B Sweet dreams

Perfect for a long weekend or an overnight stay, this small house is in the middle of spectacular countryside. Recommended for those with their own car so you can see the main sights. The organic farm nearby will provide you with the freshest produce for you to prepare the perfect meal. Reliable internet connection.

C Home away from home

Fancy a stay near the forest? Our beautiful ground-floor accommodation has three large bedrooms, a sitting room, a fully equipped kitchen and a small outdoor seating area for barbecues. Fully accessible for everyone and very convenient for the train station. We have special discounts for three-day stays which include a Saturday.

D The place

Come and enjoy the spectacular views from our affordable top-floor flat. With plenty of room for large groups and free wi-fi, our accommodation won't disappoint. Located right next to the brand-new swimming pool. You'll be able to explore most other places of interest on foot. No lift or parking.

E Number twenty-two 🔊 6.2

An awesome location! You'll be able to see the beach from the balcony. Our holiday flat is perfect for those looking for somewhere to explore the coast and perhaps have a swim. Weekends only. Nearest train station 10 kilometres away, but free parking nearby.

F Robin's nest

We've got a cosy cottage available for bookings of seven or more days. There's a large open-plan kitchen and living room downstairs, and two small bedrooms upstairs. You can also use the garage to keep things. Located on a cycle route, the nearest safe beach is an easy 10-minute ride away.

G 15A Rogers Street

If you're looking for reasonably priced accommodation for a short break, look no further. With room for six friends, this flat is conveniently located two minutes from the underground station. No need to bring the car! Please note that this is an internet-free zone.

H The guesthouse

Situated above our award-winning restaurant, our guesthouse is suitable for up to four guests. Included in the price is a special meal which we'll serve upstairs. During the day, there are plenty of walking routes for the more adventurous starting from the front gate. Book for any weekday and get 10% off.

GRAMMAR

CAN FOR ABILITY

1 Watch the grammar vlog. What's new in Alex's room?

▶ 02

2 Complete the grammar rules with *past*, *present* or *future*.

> **can for ability**
>
> 1 When we are talking about ability in the _____, we generally use *can* or *can't* + infinitive without *to*.
>
> 2 When we are talking about ability in the _____, we use *will be able to* + infinitive.
>
> 3 When we are talking about general ability in the _____, we generally use *could* or *couldn't* + infinitive without *to*. However, when we are describing ability at a specific time in the _____, we use *was/were able to* or *couldn't*.
>
> ▶ Grammar reference and practice page 119

3 Go to the digital activities.

4 Complete the text using the correct form of *can* or *be able to* and the verbs in brackets.

A FAVOURITE ARTIST

Above my bed, you [1] _____ (see) a picture by one of my favourite artists, Georgia O'Keefe. At school, her teachers realised that she [2] _____ (draw and paint) well. When she left school, she [3] _____ (get) a place at the Art Institute of Chicago and then at the Art Students League in New York. She learned traditional art techniques and with one of her paintings, she [4] _____ (win) an important prize. However, she realised she [5] _____ (not earn) enough money from being a painter and so she became a commercial artist. During a summer school, she was introduced to Modernism, where artists [6] _____ (communicate) ideas and feelings through paintings, and O'Keefe's journey as an artist began. In her 90s, although she [7] _____ (not see well), she [8] _____ (still / produce) some amazing pictures. There's going to be a huge exhibition of her work soon, I hope I [9] _____ (go).

5 Work in pairs. Take turns to ask your partner about their talents and abilities. Use the words below or your own ideas.

> cook a meal   dance or sing well
> play a musical instrument
> speak several languages

A: *Could you play the guitar when you were younger?*

B: *Yes, I could. I could play it when I was seven.*

>>> STRETCH! We can also use *manage to*, *succeed in* and *achieve* in the past instead of *be able to*. Write a paragraph about an important architect, interior designer or artist and talk about their achievements.

SPEAKING

GIVING PERSONAL OR FACTUAL INFORMATION

1 Read the Speaking Part 1 questions and think about your answers.

1 What's your name? How old are you?

2 Where do you live? Who do you live with?

3 Which do you like best, the morning or the afternoon?

4 Tell us something about your home.

2 ◁)) 6.3 Listen to Ana and Marco doing Speaking Part 1. Do they follow the advice in the exam tip box? How does the examiner repeat the question?

☑ EXAM TASK SPEAKING PART 1

> **EXAM TIP**
>
> Listen carefully to the examiner's question. If you don't understand, you can ask the examiner politely to say it again. The examiner may repeat the same question or ask it in a different way. Don't forget to answer the question in full sentences using words like *and*, *so* and *because*.

3 Work in pairs and take turns to ask and answer the questions in Exercise 1. Listen to your partner's answers.

4 Give your partner some feedback. Did your partner follow the advice in the exam tip box?

HOW IS UNIT 6 SO FAR?

☆☆☆ I understand   ☆☆ I'm getting there   ☆ I don't understand

My week living in a Stone Age camp

by teen blogger Jen Chong   Added 2 days ago

While most teenagers dream of living in an ultra-modern house, my parents took me off to a Stone Age camp. The Stone Age is, of course, the earliest period of human culture and thousands of years old. People used tools made of stone and used to move around searching for food. I was about to find out all about them.

On day one, we were given clothes which were made of animal skin and fur. Then we were shown how to build a neolithic hut. No power tools in sight, we used our hands and equipment made of wood and stone. Within two hours, I was covered in dirt, but I couldn't find a water tap to wash myself. I was directed to a freezing stream! I also washed my jacket as best as I could and hung it on a clothesline which I had made out of a branch.

As the week continued, we learned how to live without all sorts of things. Stone Age people ate animal meat, plants and fruit. Instead of putting on the kettle, we built a fire and boiled water for cooking. We didn't need a rubbish bin because nothing came in packets! I missed taking photos with my phone, but I was also happy not to hear its alarm!

Nights were a challenge without a light bulb, torch or even a candle. After an evening of storytelling, we managed to find our way back to our hut by lighting sticks.

READING

A BLOG POST

1 Work in pairs. What can you see in the photo? What would be the advantages and disadvantages of living in a place like this?

2 🔊 6.4 Read and listen to the blog post. What advantages and disadvantages does Jen Chong mention?

3 Answer the questions in your own words.

1 Why did Stone Age people not stay in one place for long?
2 What happened when Jen built her first house?
3 How did Jen make hot drinks at the camp?
4 Why did Jen mention 'packets'?
5 What did Jen find difficult when it got dark?

4 Work in pairs. Student A, you would like to stay at a Stone Age camp. Student B, you would prefer to stay in an ultra-modern house. Try to persuade your partner that you are right.

VOCABULARY

HOUSEHOLD OBJECTS

1 🔊 6.5 Go to the digital activity and match the words to the photos. Listen, check and repeat.

alarm   bin   box of matches   candle   clothesline

kettle   light bulb   tap   tools   torch

▶ Vocabulary reference page 66

2 Read the descriptions and write the objects. Use the words in Exercise 1.

1 It's usually made of metal. You push or turn it to get water.
2 You set this to wake up early or to remember to do something.
3 You can use this to find your way when it's dark.
4 It's used for rubbish.
5 We hang our wet clothes on this to dry.
6 We use these to make or repair something.

3 PRONUNCIATION Go to the digital pronunciation activity.

4 Creative Thinking Work in pairs. Choose four objects in Exercise 1 and describe their normal use. Then think of at least three alternative uses for each one.

5 You are going to spend a week at a Stone Age camp. Work in pairs and decide which of the household objects in Exercise 1 you would like to take with you. What extra item would you like to take with you? Why?

>>> STRETCH! Make a list of 6–8 modern technology objects. Which could you live without? Which could you not live without? Work in pairs and compare your ideas.

GRAMMAR

PRESENT AND PAST PASSIVE

1 Watch the grammar animation. What did Hassan forget to do?

▶ 03

2 Choose the correct words to complete the grammar rules.

> **Present and past passive**
> We use the verb in the passive:
> 1 when we are more interested in who or what *does the action / the action affects*.
> 2 when we *know / don't know* who or what did the action.
> 3 when who or what does or causes the action is *unimportant / important*.
>
> ▶ Grammar reference and practice page 119

3 📱 Go to the digital activities.

4 Complete the conversation with the correct active or passive form of the verbs in brackets. Use the past or present tense.

Helen: Have you got a favourite object in your room?

Josh: It could be this gold cat.

Helen: Where ¹ _____ (you / get) it?

Josh: It ² _____ (give) to me years ago by my aunt. I think she ³ _____ (bring) it back from one of her trips. It ⁴ _____ (call) *maneki-neko* in Japanese. People ⁵ _____ (think) it's waving, but it's actually inviting you to come nearer. The story goes that a Samurai ⁶ _____ (save) by a cat during a storm. The Samurai was standing under a tree and the cat ⁷ _____ (ask) him to come inside with its paw. Seconds later, the tree ⁸ _____ (strike) by lightning.

Helen: Cool story! Why ⁹ _____ (be / you) so fond of it?

Josh: Good question! It ¹⁰ _____ (remind) me of my aunt and of course, it ¹¹ _____ (suppose) to bring good luck.

>>> STRETCH! We can use *have something done* (or *get something done* in informal situations) when we ask other people to do things for us. Write a list of things you often *have* or *get done* and then write some sentences in the correct tense with a time expression, for example, *I got my hair cut last week, I'll get my bike repaired next week*, etc.

> **DIGITAL CLASSROOM**
> PRACTICE EXTRA UNIT 6

ORACY

Using appropriate gestures and body language

Did you know that the most viral videos online are those where the presenter speaks with their words and their hands? Using some gestures not only helps explain complicated things but also helps the listener to remember what you said. Scientists have also found that gestures make people pay attention to how the words sound.

> **Use hand gestures to talk about:**
> • size • shape • direction

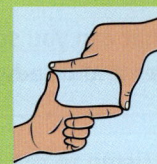

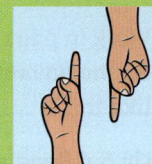

5 Work in pairs and take turns to describe something in the classroom. <u>Don't</u> use your hands or say the name of the object. Can your partner guess the object?

6 Describe another object. This time you can use your hands and other gestures. Can your partner guess the object now?

7 Discuss the questions with a partner and reflect on Exercises 5 and 6.

1 Do you often use gestures when you speak?
2 Which exercise did you find easier as the speaker? Why?
3 Which exercise did you find easier as the listener? Why?

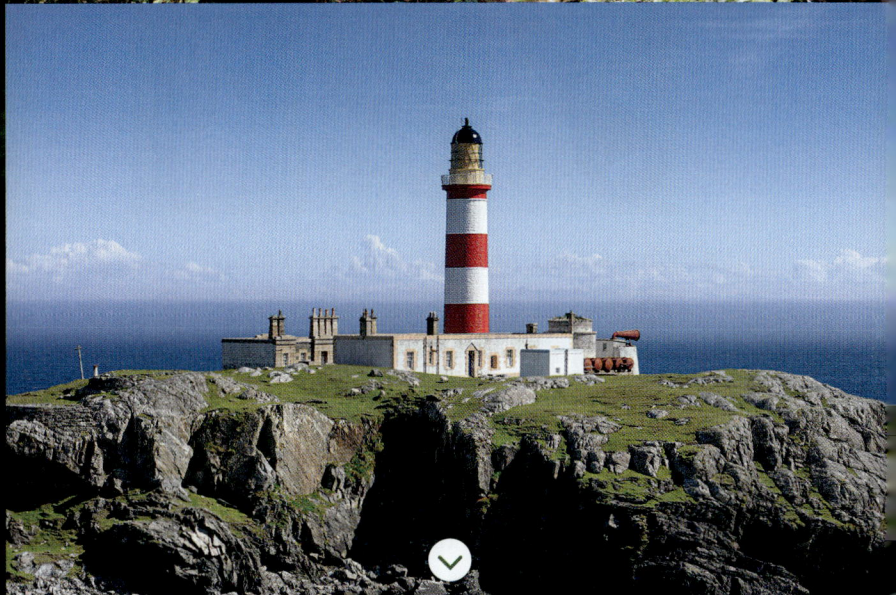

Awesome places to stay!

Martin's HANG-OUT

SOUTHEAST ENGLAND

Providing luxury accommodation for up to six guests, this property is located minutes from the cliffs and is close to the train station. On the ground floor, there's a bright kitchen with plenty of cupboards and the usual equipment – a washing machine, dishwasher, microwave, etc. The living room comes with two comfortable sofas, a smart TV and a dining area.

Upstairs there are three double bedrooms, all of them with their own bathroom. From this floor, fifteen narrow steps will take you up to the top of the tower where you can enjoy stunning views of the coast. Outside, you'll have full access to the garden with its own seating area. We've even had a barbecue and hot tub installed!

The whole building has got central heating in winter and air conditioning in summer. There is a reliable internet connection throughout. Book early to avoid disappointment!

Check dates

WRITING

A DESCRIPTION OF A PLACE

1 Look at the photos. Would you like to stay in either of these places? Why? / Why not?

2 Read a description of one of the places in the photos. Which one is it?

3 Read the description again. What information does it include? Does it include anything else?

1 price
2 location
3 number of rooms
4 transport options
5 views
6 other facilities

4 These things are used to make the property sound more attractive. Find <u>one</u> example of each in the description.

1 positive adjectives
2 things that are important for all types of people
3 cool extras
4 a sentence that sounds urgent

5 Find a photo of somewhere unusual to stay and write a description to attract guests. Use the description in Exercise 2 to help you.

6 Read your description again and revise your work. Use these questions to help you.

1 Have you included all the important information in your description? Is it well organised?
2 Have you used the techniques in Exercise 4 to make your property sound more attractive?
3 Have you used a range of language (vocabulary, *can* for ability, passives, etc.)?
4 Can you see any problems with the language (spelling, grammar, etc.)?

7 Now work in pairs. Read each other's descriptions and give feedback. Use the questions in Exercise 6 to help you. Make a note of your partner's feedback and write a second draft of your description.

8 Display the descriptions. Which place(s) would you like to stay in? Why?

9 Read the model answer.

LISTENING

MONOLOGUES AND DIALOGUES

1 **Read the questions and <u>underline</u> the key words.**

1 Where does the girl live now?

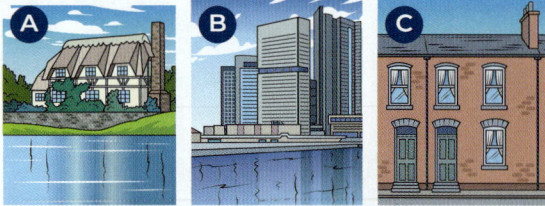

A   B   C

2 Where will the museum guide take the visitors next?

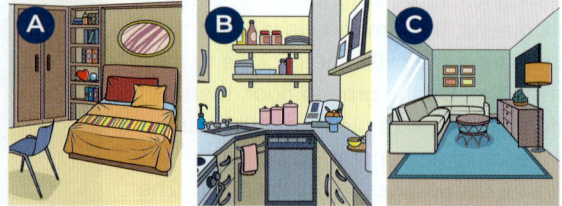

A   B   C

3 What does the girl need to buy?

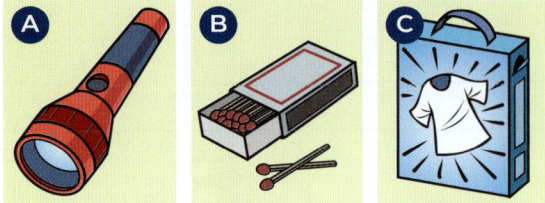

A   B   C

4 What is on special offer today?

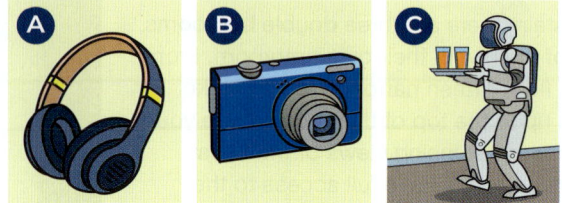

A   B   C

5 What is the school having repaired today?

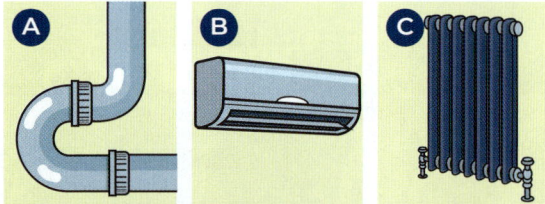

A   B   C

6 What did the girl manage to do yesterday?

A   B   C

7 Where did the man leave his watch?

A   B   C

2 **Now look at each set of pictures. What do they tell you about what you will hear?**

☑ **EXAM TASK** **LISTENING PART 1**

EXAM TIP

The information you need to answer each question may come at the beginning, in the middle or at the end. Remember to listen carefully to the <u>whole</u> recording.

3 🔊 **6.6 Listen. For each question, choose the correct answer.**

4 🔊 **6.6 Listen again and check your answers.**

5 **Work in pairs. How often do you lose things around the house? Where do you usually leave them?**

ORACY

GIVING A TALK

- sequencing ideas for structure
- using appropriate gestures and body language
- engaging the audience

1 Work in pairs. How do you feel about giving a talk? What do you think makes a talk interesting?

2 You are going to watch students planning a talk. Do they mention any of the things you talked about?

 ▶ 04

ORACY

Engaging the audience

If you don't attract your audience's attention, they may stop listening. Ways to keep people listening are to raise or lower your voice, say something funny or even ask a question.

3 ▶ 05 Now watch the group giving their talk. Who do you think feels more confident? Who is less confident?

4 🔲 Collaboration ▶ 06 Work in pairs and talk about the advice you could give members of the group to help them improve when giving a talk. Then watch the group reflecting on their talk. Is the feedback supportive? Give reasons for your opinions and actively listen to your partner's ideas.

5 Now prepare to give a talk. Choose an interesting place to talk about.

6 Plan your talk.

- Decide on a topic.
- Make some notes and include some sequencers.
- Think about your gestures and how you are going to engage your audience.
- You can either record your talk or rehearse your talk and give a live presentation.

7 Take turns to present your talk. While you listen to the others, write some notes so that you can give some supportive feedback.

8 Reflect on how well the talk went by completing the oracy checklist.

	Me	1. ____	2. ____
sequencing ideas for structure			
using appropriate gestures and body language			
engaging the audience			

9 Work in small groups. Take turns to share your reflections in Exercise 9 and give each other some supportive feedback.

SELF-ASSESSMENT: UNIT 6

How confident do you feel about:

- matching descriptions of people to short texts?
- identifying key information in short monologues or dialogues?
- responding to questions by giving personal or factual information?
- writing an attractive description of a place?
- talking about ability in the past, present or future?
- describing who or what an action affects using the passive?
- using words and phrases to talk about houses and household objects?
- giving a talk?

What was your favourite part of Unit 6? Tell your partner.

DIGITAL CLASSROOM
PERSONALISED LEARNING

VOCABULARY REFERENCE

HOUSE AND HOME

1 Find these things in the pictures. Can you find the other words in your own home?

basin   bedside table   blind   chest of drawers   curtain   duvet
fan   ground/first/second   pipe   upstairs/downstairs

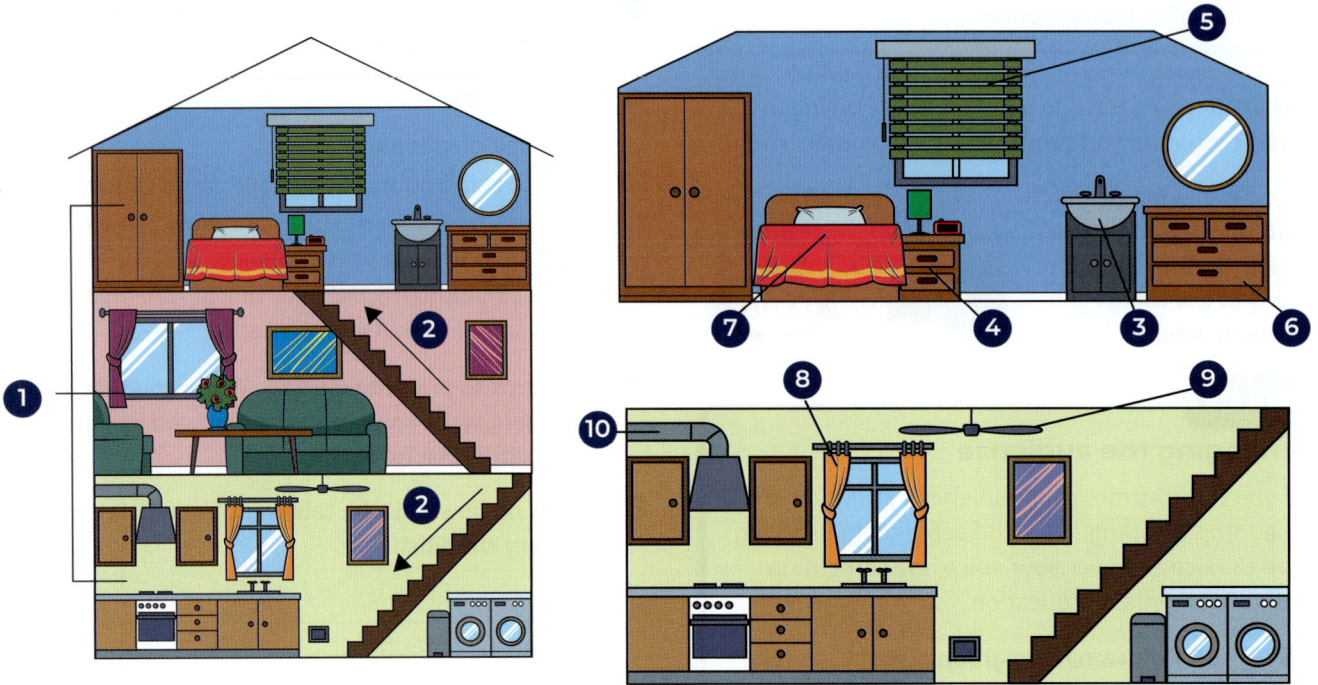

HOUSEHOLD OBJECTS

2 Match the words to the photos. Which of the objects could you live without?

alarm   bin   box of matches   candle   clothesline   kettle   light bulb   tap   tools   torch

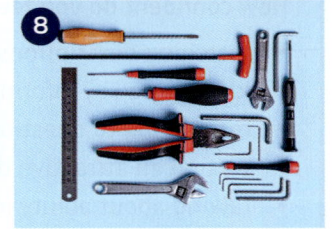

DIGITAL CLASSROOM
PRACTICE EXTRA UNIT 6

UNIT 7 EDUCATION

LEARNING AIMS

- **Skills:** discuss and create texts about education
- **Grammar:** learn and practise ways to talk about future possibility (*will*, *may* and *might*) and deductions (*must*, *may*, *might*, *could* and *can't*)
- **Vocabulary:** learn and practise words and phrases for education and collocations
- **Creative thinking:** find solutions to issues with school
- **Exam practice:** Reading Part 4, Speaking Part 2, Writing Part 2, Listening Part 4

THE CHALLENGE

Some students feel that school is boring and irrelevant for their future.

You will:

- **Stage 1 Think:** find out what students in your school think.
- **Stage 2 Prepare:** research some alternative ideas.
- **Stage 3 Develop:** decide together on the best solutions.
- **Stage 4 Present:** present your ideas.

1 **Look at the photo. Discuss the questions in small groups.**

1   What can you see in the photo?
2   How are the people feeling? Why?
3   Who can't we see in the photo? How do you think they're feeling?

2 **Watch the video. How does your school compare with those in the video?**

▶ 01

CHALLENGE ① ② ③ ④

Think

Discuss the questions with a partner and make notes.

1   What do young people often say about school?
2   What do you and your partner think about your school?
3   Can you think of any ways you could improve it?

VOCABULARY

EDUCATION

1 🖥️ 🔊 **7.1 Go to the digital activity and match the words to the photos. Listen, check and repeat.**

academic results   campus   compulsory education

grade   gym   instructor   laboratory   period

revision   tutor

▶ Vocabulary reference page 76

2 Complete this table with the words in Exercise 1. Then work in pairs and add at least three more words to the first three columns.

Person	Place	Tests	Other
			compulsory education period

3 Complete the conversation with the correct form of some of the words in Exercise 1.

Oliver: What's your school like?

Judi: It's huge! There are 1,000 students, 50 classrooms, a great ¹____ for PE and the new chemistry ²____ is excellent. We've got two ³____, one for primary and the other for secondary.

Oliver: Cool! What's your timetable like?

Judi: We have six ⁴____ a day, four before lunch and two after.

Oliver: Have you got a favourite teacher?

Judi: I like our ⁵____ because she takes an interest in our lives. She always asks us how we are. The swimming ⁶____ is cool, too! He knows how to encourage us to do our best!

Oliver: How do you feel about things like tests?

Judi: I don't really like them even though I often get good ⁷____, but that's because I do a lot of ⁸____.

4 🖥️ **PRONUNCIATION** **Go to the digital pronunciation activity.**

5 Work in pairs and ask and answer the questions in Exercise 3. Try to use some of the words in Exercise 1 in your answers.

>>> STRETCH! Look at your school timetable. Can you name all the subjects in English?

6 ▶️ **01 Watch the video again. Why are these numbers mentioned?**

1	4	5	14	18
45	60	58,000		

7 Read the questions and write down your answers. Use one or two words.

1 How many students should be in every class?
2 What is the best age to start school?
3 How much homework should students get a week?
4 How long should high school students spend at school a day?

8 🔊 **7.2 Listen to Talia and Erik. Which question in Exercise 7 do they discuss?**

ORACY

Using evidence

Use evidence to support your argument and convince others that you are right.

9 🔊 **7.2 Now listen again. Which of these phrases do Talia and Erik use?**

But this source puts that in …
Does it mention …?
It goes on to say …
There's strong evidence that …
This information comes from …
This source looks reliable.
This website says that …

10 Work in small groups and choose at least two of the questions in Exercise 7. Look at your own answer. Do some online research to find some evidence to support your opinion.

11 Discuss your ideas and reach an agreement. Use the expressions in Exercise 9 to do this.

🛡️ CHALLENGE ─①─②─③─④

Prepare

1 Form groups of three or four people.
2 Choose one of the most common opinions about school.
3 Design a questionnaire to find out about what students really think and give it to students in your school.
4 Look at the results and decide how you will look for solutions.

MY SCHOOL YEAR IN FINLAND

a blog post by Callie Matthews

🔊 7.3

I let my friends know on social media that I've arrived and I'm about to begin my first day. 'That must be a challenge, Callie!' one of my friends has just posted. Before I left, I worried about everything. [1] _____ I don't know why I was nervous. I'm having an amazing time!

It's 9.30 am on day one and I'm greeted at the front gate by the head teacher and my form tutor. I can hear you all saying, 'That's late!' [2] _____ We have longer lessons, fewer periods, much better breaks in between and lunch at home. My form tutor explains that having more time gives us an opportunity to explore a subject in more detail.

Two of my new classmates appear to give me a brief tour. They introduce themselves and say, 'You must have loads of questions.' Of course, I do. I begin and I can't stop. 'Will there be tests? How much homework will we get? Will I have to study a lot?' [3] _____ There won't be important tests, but the teacher will give us a grade for our progress. Sometimes we might get homework, but students in Finland do less work outside class than any other country in the world. [4] _____ I can't believe how lucky I am!

Something else becomes obvious as I listen to these two: the Finnish school system is based on cooperation and collaboration rather than competition. The school and its teachers aren't trying to be the best in the world. The students aren't either. [5] _____ My two new friends have managed to make me feel at home and I'm already looking forward to getting to class.

READING

A BLOG

1 Work in small groups. You are going to spend a school year abroad. What do you think you will enjoy about the experience? What will the challenges be?

2 Read Callie's blog post. What is different about her new school? Do not complete the gaps for now.

3 Some of these sentences have been removed from the blog post. Do you think the words in bold refer to a teacher, a student, a group of students or a situation?

A **Some of them** study hard outside class to get good grades.

B **They both** start laughing, tell me to calm down and say it's the first day.

C **That** means we eat in the canteen at midday.

D **None of them** sign up for after-school classes either.

E **This** included the fact that I might find everything too difficult and I won't understand anything.

F **Nobody** worries about coming top of the class.

G **This** doesn't mean we finish later: the day ends at 2.30.

H **He** tells me not to worry about anything and to enjoy myself.

✓ **EXAM TASK**   READING PART 4

4 Five of the sentences in Exercise 4 have been removed from the blog post. For each question, choose the correct answer (A–H). There are three extra sentences which you do not need to use.

5 🔵 Emotional Development Work in small groups. A student from Finland is going to spend a year in your school. What will they find different? How can you support them and help them adapt?

GRAMMAR

FUTURE POSSIBILITY (*WILL, MAY* AND *MIGHT*)

1 Watch the grammar vlog. What does Leo say about schools in the future? Do you agree with his ideas? ▶ 02

2 Complete the grammar rules with *will*, *won't*, *may* or *might*.

> **Future possibility (*will*, *may* and *might*)**
>
> When we talk about possibility in the future, we use:
>
> 1 _____ with the infinitive when something is sure to happen in the future.
>
> 2 _____ or _____ with the infinitive when something is possible but not certain.
>
> 3 _____ with the infinitive if something is impossible.
>
> ▶ Grammar reference and practice page 120

3 🖥 Go to the digital activities.

4 Complete the comments with *may*, *will* or *won't* and one of the verbs.

> be (x3)   change   close   give   have to   start

Roz, 14
@RJRyan · Follow

What do you think your school
¹ _____ like in the future?

Pete, 12   @PtrPan

I'm sure our school ² _____ a lot in the future. There are fewer children in our neighbourhood, so there ³ _____ as many pupils as now. They ⁴ _____ one of the campuses, but it isn't certain.

Misha, 15   @Mish_15

Our school gym is really old, so they definitely ⁵ _____ build a new one.

Zuri, 11   @ZZuriii

I hope teachers ⁶ _____ students less homework and tests and it ⁷ _____ difficult to get good grades.

Nicki, 13   @Nicola0108

I'm not certain but I think compulsory education ⁸ _____ earlier so that there's somewhere for small children to go.

5 Work in pairs. Write at least four predictions about schools in the future. Use these ideas or your own ideas.

> homework and tests   lessons on demand
> school buildings or online lessons
> science laboratories and virtual reality
> the range of school subjects
> the role of the teacher

6 🎓 **Critical Thinking** Work in pairs. Find some reliable sources which either agree or disagree with your predictions in Exercise 5. Make notes.

7 Work in small groups. Choose the more reliable predictions and report back to the whole class on what you found.

>>> STRETCH! Choose an area which interests you, for example sport, entertainment, food, etc. and write two or three predictions. Then use reliable sources to see if your predictions could come true. Report back to the class.

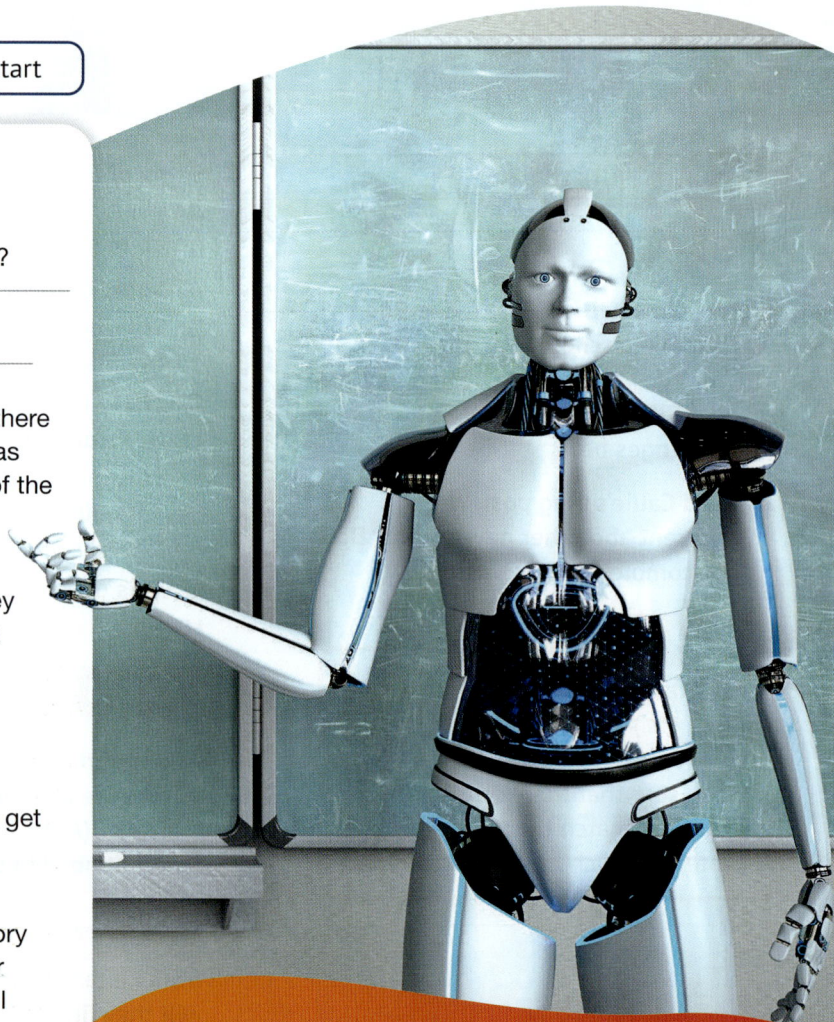

HOW IS UNIT 7 SO FAR?

☆☆☆☆ I understand   ☆☆☆ I'm getting there   ☆ I don't understand

WHY DO I ENJOY SCHOOL?

THINK OUTSIDE THE BOX!

by Malik, aged 16

Imagine a school where you have to take a difficult test which includes a live performance to get a place. In the summer holiday, you attend a compulsory two-week training camp. Then, when the term starts, you're there 24/7 apart from when you break up for Christmas. And on top of all that, you sleep in the school's accommodation. You're probably thinking that must be hard. You may even wonder why anyone goes to that school. In actual fact, 30 of us go there and we love it! Let me tell you why.

We go to the drama school in our province. So, how does it work? Our school timetable must look very much like yours. We do all the typical subjects like English, Spanish, maths, science and technology for around 25 hours a week. For the other 18 hours, we do singing, dance and acting with the most amazing instructors who really know about performing.

Our day ends at 6.30 pm and we go back to the accommodation. We can use the library, there are plenty of computers and there's always somebody around to help us with our homework or revise for a test. The school also organises cultural activities and trips.

It's funny, at my old school, I wasn't a good student. I didn't use to work hard and I used to fail exams. Now I'm doing really well. I know I need to study hard to get my high school diploma, but once I get that, I can become a professional performer.

MEDIATION WORKSHEET

READING

A BLOG POST

1 🔊 7.4 Read and listen to Malik's blog post. Why does he enjoy school?

2 Answer the questions in your own words.

   1 Why do people think that Malik's school must be hard?
   2 In what ways is Malik's school timetable similar and different to yours?
   3 Does Malik get homework? How do you know?
   4 How has Malik changed as a student? Why?

3 **Creative Thinking** What type of school would you like to go to? Would it be for clowns, skateboarders, rappers or perhaps something else? Use your imagination!

VOCABULARY

COLLOCATIONS

1 📱 🔊 7.5 Go to the digital activity and look at the photos. How many of these words can you find? Then listen to all the words and repeat.

do well/badly   break up   fail/pass an exam
get a place (to study) at (college/university)
know about something   revise for a test
sit/take an exam

▶ Vocabulary reference page 76

2 Work in pairs and put the events in Exercise 1 into a logical order to make a short story.

Tom revised for his test and …

3 Work in small groups. What do you think of these ideas? Try to use some of the collocations in Exercise 1.

being allowed to take your books/notes into tests

no homework at all

a year abroad before university

longer school holidays

more marks for attendance and behaviour

ORACY

Summarising

To report a group discussion, think about the most important points and any conclusions and then prepare a short summary.

4 🔊 7.6 Listen to the summary of a group's discussion in Exercise 3. In what order do you hear these phrases?

   a One of us suggested that we should …
   b We didn't all share the same opinion about …
   c Our group talked about …
   d Our group came to the conclusion that …
   e We all agree that … because …
   f Two people feel it's a good thing because …
   g … while the others believe …

5 Work in your groups from Exercise 3 and produce a summary of your discussion. Use the phrases in Exercise 4 to help you.

GRAMMAR

MODAL VERBS OF DEDUCTION (*MUST, MAY, MIGHT, COULD, CAN'T*)

1 Watch the grammar animation. Where is Chris's lucky pencil? ▶ 03

2 Choose the correct words to complete the grammar rules.

> **Modal verbs of deduction (*must, may, might, could, can't*)**
>
> We can use *must, may, might, could* and *can't* with an infinitive to talk about probability.
>
> 1 When we think something is certain or *probable / possible*, we use *must*.
> 2 When we think something is *probable / possible*, we use *may, might* or *could*.
> 3 When we think something is *possible / impossible*, we use *can't*.
> 4 We don't use *can* to talk about probability.
>
> ▶ Grammar reference and practice page 120

3 🖥 Go to the digital activities.

4 Read the situation and answer the question. Use *must, can't, may, might* or *could* and a suitable verb.

1 Your teacher asks where Liam is. You saw him in the canteen five minutes ago. What do you say?
   He might be in the canteen. I saw him there five minutes ago.
2 Your friend asks about the weather. Everyone's wearing thick coats outside. What do you say?
3 Your sister asks if there's pizza for dinner. It's Friday and you always have fish on Fridays. What do you say?
4 There's a new restaurant but it's empty for most of the day. What do you think?
5 You see a close friend in town but she doesn't stop to say hello. Why?

SPEAKING

DESCRIBING A PHOTO

1 Look at the photos on this page. Which of these things could you describe?

1	activities	2	clothes
3	colours	4	objects
5	people	6	place
7	time of day	8	weather

2 Watch a candidate describing one of the photos. Which photo does she describe? Which of the things in Exercise 1 does she describe? ▶ 04

☑ EXAM TASK SPEAKING PART 2

> **EXAM TIP**
>
> Imagine you're describing the photo to someone who can't see it. You should describe everything, including the colours, place, time of day, people, etc.

3 Work in pairs. Student A, choose one of the photos on the page and describe it without showing it to your partner. Student B, listen and say which photo your partner described.

4 Now swap roles.

5 Work in pairs and discuss the questions.

1 Did you manage to speak for one minute?
2 Did you follow the exam tip?
3 How could you make your description even better?

🛡 CHALLENGE ─ 1 2 3 4

Develop

1 Decide what solutions you want to present.
2 Decide how you will present them, for example, in a short video or in an infographic.
3 Create a first draft.

WRITING

AN ARTICLE

1 You see this announcement in an online magazine. What would you write in your article?

ARTICLES WANTED FOR OUR
NEW SCHOOL MAGAZINE!

What makes a great teacher?

Is it their knowledge of the subject, their ability to teach or is it something else?

The best articles will be published in our first edition next month.

---

2 Read Georgia's article. Do you agree with her? Why? / Why not?

What makes a great teacher?

Could it be an expert who knows their stuff? Or might it be somebody who prepares fantastic lessons **in** ¹ ____? It's true that students expect their history teacher, for example, to know their facts or their IT teacher to be **up to** ² ____ with the latest technology. I also prefer someone who arrives **on** ³ ____, is enjoyable to listen to and who pauses **at** ⁴ ____ every few minutes to allow students to ask questions.

However, I also feel that being friendly and kind is essential. If a teacher doesn't greet everyone **at** ⁵ ____ the lesson, we may think they're angry with us. **At** ⁶ ____ time, I believe that a teacher should know all their students **by** ⁷ ____.

3 Complete the phrases with prepositions in Georgia's article in Exercise 2 with the words.

> advance   date   least   name
> the beginning of   the same   time

4 Read the article again and answer the questions. Use examples from the text to support your answer.

1 Does the article have a title? Is it divided into paragraphs?
2 Does the article answer the questions in Exercise 1?
3 Does Georgia give her opinion?
4 Is the article interesting to read? Why? / Why not?

EXAM TIP

Remember to attract your reader's attention from the beginning by asking questions so that they will want to keep reading.

5 Work in pairs. Look at the exam task below and discuss the questions.

1 What do you think makes a great student?
2 What information will you include in the first paragraph?
3 What information will you include in the second paragraph?

You see this announcement in an English-language magazine.

Articles wanted!

What makes a great student?

Is it their knowledge of the subjects, their ability to study or is it something else?

The best articles will be published next month.

---

6 Look at Georgia's article in Exercise 2. How does she attract the reader's attention? How could you do this in your own article?

7 Write your article in 100 words. Use Georgia's article to help you.

8 Read your article again and revise it. Use these questions to help you.

1 Does the article have a title and is it divided into paragraphs?
2 Does the article answer the questions in the announcement?
3 Do you attract attention from the beginning by asking questions?
4 Is there a range of language, including some phrases with prepositions?
5 Can you see any problems with the language (spelling, grammar, etc.)?

9 Now work in pairs. Read each other's articles and give feedback. Use the questions in Exercise 8 to help you. Make a note of your partner's feedback and write a second draft of your article.

10 🔲 Read the model answer.

AN INTERVIEW

1 **Work in pairs and answer the questions.**

1 What does a language assistant do?
2 Have you ever had an assistant in your language class? What did they do?

2 **You will hear an interview with a woman called Bimpe who is talking about her job as a language assistant. Read the questions or statements (1–6) and underline the key words. Then do the same for the options A, B and C.**

1 What language(s) is Bimpe good at?
   A English only
   B English and French only
   C English, French and Yoruba

2 When Bimpe was at school, she felt
   A her teacher was laughing at her.
   B she had to do well in French.
   C lucky to speak languages.

3 Why did Bimpe become a language assistant?
   A It was part of her university degree.
   B She wanted to take some time off.
   C Her mum told her to do it.

4 What did Bimpe do at the secondary school?
   A She encouraged the students to communicate in English.
   B She taught the students some French vocabulary.
   C She showed the students how to write good questions.

5 During her time at the school, Bimpe
   A interviewed a few students for her research.
   B took some of the students to her old school.
   C helped the students learn more about her country.

6 What did Bimpe like best about being an English-language teaching assistant?
   A spending time in Paris
   B being told nice things
   C getting to know new people

✓ EXAM TASK **LISTENING PART 4**

EXAM TIP

You may hear information connected to all three options, but remember only one answer is correct.

3 🔊 **7.7 Now listen to the recording. For each question, choose the correct answer.**

4 🔊 **7.8 Now listen to part of the interview again and complete the interviewer's second question.**

Interviewer: _____! _____, did you do anything else with them?

5 **Why does the interviewer use the comment and question in Exercise 4? Check your ideas with the information in the oracy tip below.**

ORACY

Listening actively

When someone takes a longer turn at speaking, for example, when they develop their opinion, it's good to know that the listener is paying attention. Respond with follow-up questions and comments to show that you are listening actively.

6 **Work in groups and talk about whether you would like to be a language assistant. Give reasons. Remember to show that you are listening actively to each other by responding with follow-up questions and using some of these comments.**

Sounds interesting!   Really?   That's a good point!
I'd never thought of that!   Go on!
What do you mean exactly?

🛡 CHALLENGE ⟨1⟩–⟨2⟩–⟨3⟩–⟨4⟩

Present

1 Make sure you have everything you need for your presentation.
2 Check that the information in your first draft is clear and everyone in your group knows what they have to do.
3 Create a second draft.
4 Present your solutions to your class. For example, play your video or explain your infographic.

WRAP UP

Look back at the unit. Write down:

① some new vocabulary you learned to talk about school.

② your main role in the challenge.

③ the difference between *will/won't* and *may/might* to describe future possibility.

④ the difference between modal verbs of deduction: *must, may, might, could* and *can't*.

⑤ something in the unit that you especially enjoyed.

⟳ Sustainability

1 Think of a sustainable idea that your class could implement to take care of the environment at your school.

2 How could you and your classmates help to implement this idea?

SELF-ASSESSMENT: UNIT 7

How confident do you feel about:

- completing an article with missing sentences?
- describing a photo for one minute?
- writing an interesting article?
- listening to an interview and answering multiple-choice questions?
- using *will*, *may*, *might* and *won't* to describe future possibility?
- using *must*, *may*, *might*, *could* and *can't* to talk about future probability?
- talking about your school and the activities you do there?
- finding out about what students think, researching ideas and presenting solutions?

What was your favourite part of Unit 7? Tell your partner.

🛡 **Emotional Development** Have you helped someone in need lately at school? What did your classmate need? What kind of support did you offer? How did it make you feel?

⟫ STRETCH! YOUR CHOICE

Now, choose an option.

Option 1:
Make a video about your school for new students. Include useful information, your own top tips and also some unusual facts. Show your video to your teacher and class and ask for feedback.

Option 2:
Do some research into education around the world, focusing on specific areas such as the school leaving age, number of hours students study, range of school subjects, etc. Create an infographic and show it to your classmates.

Option 3:
Design a new school subject. Think about an attractive name, the content, the materials and also homework and tests. Present your ideas to the class.

VOCABULARY REFERENCE

EDUCATION

1 Match the words to the photos.

academic results   campus   compulsory education   grade
gym   instructor   laboratory   period   revision   tutor

DIGITAL CLASSROOM
PRACTICE EXTRA UNIT 7

COLLOCATIONS

2 Look at the photos. How many of the words can you find?

do well/badly   break up   fail/pass an exam   get a place (to study) at (college/university)
know about something   sit/take an exam   revise for a test

UNIT 8 THE BEST WEATHER

LEARNING AIMS

Skills: discuss and create texts about weather and outdoor activities

Grammar: learn and practise the first conditional, the zero conditional and *if*, *when* and *unless*

Vocabulary: learn and practise words and phrases for the weather and outdoor equipment

Oracy: participate actively in discussions

Exam practice: Reading Part 1, Speaking Part 3, Listening Part 2

ORACY

Participating actively in discussions

• getting everyone's opinion
• taking turns
• interrupting politely

1 **Look at the photo. Discuss the questions in small groups.**

1 What kind of weather do you see?
2 How do you think weather can affect people's emotions?
3 How does the weather affect what animals do?

2 **Watch the video. What animals are mentioned?**

▶ 01

3 **In groups of three, look at the statements and select which one you would like to discuss. Talk about it together and try to reach an agreement.**

• It's best to live in a place where the weather is always the same.
• People who live in sunny places are happier.
• The weather is changing, and that's a bad thing for the world.

4 **Think about your group discussion in Exercise 3. Did you use any of the tips in the Oracy box? Which ones? Compare your answers.**

Documentary

Grammar

Grammar

Speaking

Oracy

VOCABULARY

WEATHER

1 🖥 🔊 **8.1 Go to the digital activity and match the words to the photos. Listen, check and repeat.**

a breeze   a gale   a humid day   icy conditions
lightning   a shower   snowfall   sunshine
a (thunder)storm   a rainbow

▶ Vocabulary reference page 86

2 Complete the situations in the weather quiz with the correct form of words from Exercise 1. Then tick how you would feel in each situation.

	😄	😐	😨
You're looking out the window at a dramatic ¹ ____ with flashes of ² ____ every few seconds.			
The sea is frozen and you're walking on the ice in beautiful, bright ³ ____.			
You have to be really careful where you walk because of the ⁴ ____.			
There has been heavy ⁵ ____ and now you're out having a snowball fight.			
The wind is more than a gentle ⁶ ____. It's a ⁷ ____, and you're outside with leaves and sticks flying around your ears.			
You're in a rainforest on a(n) ⁸ ____ when there is a sudden ⁹ ____ that makes your hair, clothes and shoes as wet as the sea.			
It's raining but the sun is out too, and there's a bright, colourful ¹⁰ ____ in the sky.			

3 Look at where most of your ticks are in the quiz in Exercise 2. Then read the key for you. Does it really describe you? Compare your results with a partner.

Mostly 😄: You love an adventure. Excitement is your happiness. Just please be careful! Go inside when the weather gets too bad.

Mostly 😨: You want a comfortable life and you probably love your sofa. Why not? It's important to stay safe. But maybe a little bit of excitement would make your nice life even better.

Mostly 😐: Really? Don't these situations make you feel excited or horrified? Come on, you must have an opinion! We think you should do the quiz again!

4 Think back to the video and discuss the questions in groups.

1 How often do you check the weather forecast? Why?
2 Do you think animals know better than humans what weather is coming?

5 Make a table like this one. Then ask four of your classmates the questions and fill in the table. Report back to the class.

Name	Tanya	Carlos	Sophie
What's your favourite kind of weather?			
What do you like doing in warm weather?			
What do you like doing in cold/rainy weather?			

⟫ STRETCH! What words do you know for extreme weather? Is the weather sometimes extreme where you live? Describe situations where the weather can become dangerous. Look up any words you don't know.

READING

REAL WORLD NOTICES

1 What kinds of things are sometimes cancelled because of bad weather?

✓ **EXAM TASK** READING PART 1

2 For each question, choose the correct answer.

1 **HARBOUR CLOSED.**
All boat trips cancelled today due to stormy weather conditions. 🔊 8.2

A Only boats that are safe in strong winds can enter the harbour.
B Boats cannot enter or leave the harbour for the rest of the day.
C The harbour will open later in the day if the weather gets better.

2 ← **Tobi**
Online

It's going to rain this afternoon, so we're meeting in the youth club building and not at the lake. See you all there later. Tobi.

A Tobi wants to meet his friends at a lake later today.
B Tobi will contact people again later about where to meet.
C Tobi has changed the arranged meeting place.

3 **Subject:** Students booked on camping weekend

Please remember to take a good-quality sleeping bag as temperatures can fall to below 10 degrees at night.

A Students need a sleeping bag which will keep them warm in low temperatures.
B Students should take a good bag with enough equipment for a whole weekend.
C Students who don't like cold weather should not go on the camping trip.

4
FINEST QUALITY BUTTER BISCUITS

Please keep this product in a cool, dry place and eat within three days after opening.

A If you eat the biscuits cold, they taste better.
B The biscuits won't stay good for long if they are kept in a warm place.
C Open the packet three days before you want to eat the biscuits.

5
Remember to give the cat a tin of cat food at about 7 pm and make sure she still has enough water. Thanks!

A The cat needs to be washed and fed in the evening.
B The cat must have a fresh drink in the evening.
C The cat should get a meal in the evening.

ORACY

Getting everyone's opinion

Some people find it difficult to speak in groups but they still have an opinion. Encourage them to speak by asking them for their opinion. You could also discuss ideas in pairs before you work together as a group.

3 Work in groups of five or six and discuss these ways of getting everyone's opinion in a discussion. Which do you think are the most useful?

- Have a group leader who tells people when to speak.
- Have a group leader who asks people if they want to speak.
- Let people speak in pairs before the group discussion.
- Let people write down their opinions before the group discussion.
- Show that you are listening to the speaker.
- Give positive feedback when somebody speaks.
- Ask everyone to vote on decisions.

4 In your group, choose a leader. Think about different kinds of written messages and discuss the questions below. Use some ideas from Exercise 3 to make sure everyone contributes.

1 What is the best way to invite a group of friends to a party?
2 What is the best way for teachers to inform parents of events at school?
3 What is the best way for schools to inform students about upcoming events?

GRAMMAR

FIRST CONDITIONAL

1 Watch the grammar animation. Why do Chris and Hassan change their plans for the weekend?

▶ 02

2 Complete the sentences from the grammar animation and then complete the grammar rules.

1 If it _____, we _____ in our tents.
2 You _____ them if it _____ cold at night.
3 If bears _____ food, they sometimes _____ to get inside tents.
4 But it _____ a problem if you _____ the right equipment.

> **First conditional**
>
> 1 We form the first conditional with *if* + ____ simple and a verb with ____.
> 2 We use the first conditional to talk about things which will be true or possible in the ____ if some other things happen.
> *You'll have a good time if you plan your trip well.*
> *If you don't plan well, you'll have some problems.*
>
> ▶ Grammar reference and practice page 121

3 🖥 Go to the digital activities.

4 Answer the questions in your own words.

1 What will you do next weekend if it rains?
2 What will you do if it's sunny and warm?
3 Will you be surprised if it snows at the weekend? Why? / Why not?

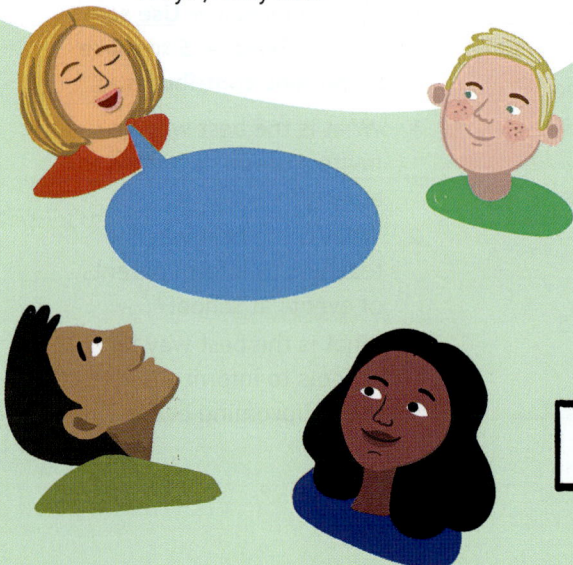

>>> STRETCH! Find out more about how scientists say the weather will change or is changing in your region. Do you think it is a problem? Why / Why not? Write a paragraph about it.

ORACY

Taking turns

It's natural that some people talk more than others, but it's also important that everyone gets a turn. You need to speak when it's your turn, and you must also know when to *stop* speaking. People might stop listening to you or interrupt if you speak for too long.

5 🔊 8.3 Listen to two discussions. Are the sentences true for Discussion 1 or Discussion 2?

1 One person talks much more than the others.
2 Speakers ask each other for opinions.
3 One person tries to take a turn but can't.
4 Turn-taking works well in this discussion.

6 In some cultures, it is not impolite for a lot of people to speak at once, but in others it is extremely rude to start speaking before another person has finished. In pairs, decide where you would put your culture on this line. Say why.

| 1 | 2 | 3 | 4 | 5 |

HOW IS UNIT 8 SO FAR?

☆☆☆☆ I understand   ☆☆ I'm getting there   ☆ I don't understand

WE L♥VE THE RAIN!

What does 'good weather' mean to you? Most people would answer 'sunshine', but not everyone. We talked to four people who love the rain.

KIRA (14): Swimming in the sea in the rain is my favourite thing ever! If the water is really cold, you can use a wetsuit, but actually, the sea often feels very warm when it rains. Stay safe, though. You need to warm up quickly when you get out of the water. Take a flask with you to the beach and have a hot drink. And never go swimming in a storm.

ELIAS (18): I love hiking in the rain. Everything smells good out in the country when it rains, and I love the sound of the rain on leaves. You have a better chance of seeing some animals, too, like frogs. You need waterproof clothes, of course, and good walking boots. In case something goes wrong, have some emergency equipment like a torch, a penknife and maybe a small first-aid kit. You'll probably never need them but it's important to respect the power of nature, and to be sensible.

THINK OUTSIDE THE BOX!

MONICA (55): Rainy weather is perfect for fishing! As soon as I see the clouds coming, I get my fishing rod and a raincoat with a hood, and I go to the lake. It's not for everyone, but if I can catch my own dinner, it makes me happy!

SIMON (5): I love puddles! When it rains, I put on my raincoat and my wellies, find the biggest puddles, and jump into them. Rain is the best weather, and you only see rainbows if it rains!

MEDIATION WORKSHEET

READING

AN ARTICLE

1 🔊 8.4 Read and listen to the article. Match the opinions (1–4) to the people.

> Kira Elias Monica Simon

1 Rainy days are best for catching lots of fish.
2 You can really enjoy nature on long walks in the rain.
3 It's great to go swimming in the rain, but don't get too cold.
4 Rain is just so much fun!

2 **Are the sentences true or false? Correct the false sentences.**

1 Kira says that sometimes when it's raining, the water in the sea doesn't feel cold.
2 She recommends going home and making a warm drink soon after your swim.
3 Elias likes the sounds and smells of nature in the rain.
4 He says you need a lot of safety equipment as hiking in the rain is dangerous.
5 Monica thinks that everybody should try fishing.
6 Simon loves going out in his waterproof clothes and having fun in the rain.

3 **What other reasons can you think of to love the rain? Work in pairs and make a list.**

4 🅖 **Creative Thinking** Is the weather in the painting good or bad? Talk to a partner about what you can see in the painting and how it makes you feel.

VOCABULARY

OUTDOOR EQUIPMENT

1 📱 🔊 8.5 Go to the digital activity and match the words to the photos. Listen, check and repeat.

> first-aid kit   fishing rod   flask   helmet
> hood   mosquito spray   penknife   torch
> walking boots   waterproof clothes
> wellington boots (wellies)   wetsuit

▶ Vocabulary reference page 86

2 **Work in pairs and decide what you would need for these activities. Use the words from Exercise 1.**

• a cycling trip   • fishing
• a walk in a rainforest

⟩⟩⟩ STRETCH! What do you do outside? Do you need any special clothes or equipment for that? Find out the English words for the things you need when you are outside.

GRAMMAR

IF, WHEN AND UNLESS

1 Watch the grammar vlog. Why is Leo interested in the weather forecast?

▶ 03

2 Choose the correct words to complete the sentences. Then complete the grammar rules with *if, when* or *unless*.

1 Leo knows he will enjoy his weekend *if / when* the weather is good.

2 Leo and his friends will buy food *if / when* they get to the coast.

3 He won't read *when / unless* he gets bored.

> **If, when and unless**
>
> 1 _____ means the same as *if not*.
> 2 We use _____ for things that may happen.
> 3 We use _____ for things that will happen.
>
> ▶ Grammar reference and practice page 121

3 🖥 Go to the digital activities.

4 Complete the second sentence so that it means the same as the first.

1 I'll go to the beach if it doesn't rain.
   I'll go to the beach _____ it rains.

2 The roads will be closed unless the snow stops soon.
   The roads will be closed if _____ stop soon.

3 You'll get wet unless you take an umbrella.
   You'll get wet if _____.

4 If he doesn't wear gloves, he'll get very cold hands.
   _____ gloves, he'll get very cold hands.

5 🖥 **PRONUNCIATION** Go to the digital pronunciation activity.

6 Complete the sentences with your own ideas. Then work in pairs and compare your sentences.

1 When I get home today, …
2 Unless I'm really bored, …
3 If my friends invite me on a boat trip, …

>>> **STRETCH!** Olivia says, 'As soon as I get back, I'll tell you all about it.' Write more first conditional sentences with *as soon as* instead of *if/when/unless*.

> **DIGITAL CLASSROOM**
> **PRACTICE EXTRA UNIT 8**

SPEAKING

MAKING AND RESPONDING TO SUGGESTIONS

1 Watch two students completing a Speaking Part 3 task. How many conditional sentences do you hear?

▶ 04

☑ **EXAM TASK** **SPEAKING PART 3**

EXAM TIP

Conditional forms are useful when you are discussing and explaining different options in the Speaking test. You will feel more confident in Part 3 if you are comfortable using conditionals.

2 Work in pairs to complete the exam task. You have two to three minutes.

A boy is leaving his school and moving to another city near the sea. His friends know he loves sport, and want to get him a goodbye present.

Here are some things they could get him.

Talk together about the different presents they could get him, and say which one would be the best.

WRITING

AN ADVICE PAGE

1 Look at the photo. Why could it be difficult to walk on this pavement? Is this a problem where you live?

2 Read the advice from a weather website and answer the questions.

1 What is 'black ice'?
2 At what temperature does it typically occur?
3 How should you walk on black ice?
4 What does the writer advise people to wear in icy conditions?

⚠ BLACK ICE safety tips

Ice on roads and pavements is dangerous, especially when it's hard to see it. 'Black ice' is completely clear, so you don't usually notice it is there until you slip. Every winter, people fall and hurt themselves on black ice, so here is our advice on how to stay safe in these conditions.

1 Know when to expect black ice. It occurs when rain hits the ground and immediately freezes. It's also a problem when snow melts and then freezes again, so you should be especially careful when the temperature is around 0 degrees Celsius.

2 Take slow and careful steps. Keep your feet near the ground when you walk, or even *on* the ground. Do you know the way that penguins walk? If you have to walk on black ice, try it! It helps a lot.

3 Wear the right shoes. You must have shoes that are suitable for winter conditions. If the bottom of your shoes are completely flat, they don't grip the ground, and you will probably slip and fall on black ice!

3 Imperatives and modal verbs are useful for giving instructions and advice. Work in pairs and find examples in the advice in Exercise 2.

1 Find three modal verbs.
2 Find five imperatives.
3 Which imperative is part of a conditional sentence?

4 Work in pairs and look at the photos on page 126. Discuss what kind of weather you can see and why that weather can be dangerous. Which kind of weather do you think is the most dangerous?

5 Pick one kind of weather condition and write a page for a weather website about it. Include:

- an introduction explaining the weather condition and why it can be dangerous.
- two or three paragraphs with advice about staying safe in this weather.

6 Read your page again and revise your work. Use these questions to help you.

1 Have you included an introduction?
2 Have you included two or three pieces of advice?
4 Have you used imperatives and modal verbs for instructions and advice?
5 Can you see any problems with the language (spelling, grammar, etc.)?

7 Now work in pairs. Read each other's pages and give feedback. Use the questions in Exercise 6 to help you. Make a note of your partner's feedback and write a second draft.

8 🖥 Read the model answer.

LISTENING

SHORT DIALOGUES

1 Work in pairs and discuss the question. What is your favourite season? Why?

✓ **EXAM TASK** LISTENING PART 2

2 🔊 **8.6** For each question, choose the correct answer.

1 You will hear two friends talking about seasons. Which season do they like the best?
   A autumn
   B summer
   C winter

2 You will hear two friends talking about their holidays. The boy is surprised because
   A the girl went to Australia.
   B the girl has family in Australia.
   C it was too cold to swim in Australia.

3 You will hear a boy telling his sister about a cycling trip. The girl says that the boy should
   A wear more comfortable sports clothes.
   B wear clothes that keep him safe on the road.
   C wear a warm jacket.

4 You will hear two friends talking about a new boy at school. What will they do to help him make friends?
   A talk to him at lunchtime
   B play football with him
   C invite him to join a school club

5 You will hear a girl talking about a film she saw. What did she like best about the film?
   A the star of the film
   B the use of technology
   C the film's story

6 You will hear a boy telling a girl about his homework. Why does he feel annoyed about it?
   A It's taking too long.
   B He's finding it too hard.
   C It isn't going to be useful for real life.

3 🎓 **Learning to Learn** Was the Listening task easy or difficult for you? Work in pairs and share and discuss any tips you can think of to help with Listening tasks.

ORACY

Interrupting politely

Sometimes you might strongly disagree with something in a discussion, or maybe another person has been speaking for much too long. In that case, you can interrupt, but make sure you do it politely. Use phrases like 'Can I interrupt for a moment?' or 'Can I just say something here?'

4 🔊 **8.7** Listen to two friends having a conversation. Read the questions and answer *the girl* or *the boy*.

1 Who interrupts because one person is speaking too much?
2 Who interrupts because he/she disagrees?
3 Who reacts positively to an interruption?
4 Who is annoyed by an interruption?

5 Share your tips for Listening tasks with another pair. Together, try to agree on your three top tips for the Listening exam. You may need to interrupt each other, so don't forget to do it politely.

ORACY

SURVIVAL GAME

- getting everyone's opinion
- taking turns
- interrupting politely

1 Watch some students talking about a speaking activity they will do. Answer the questions.

 ▶ 05

1 What decision will the group have to make in the activity?
2 What decision do they have to make now?
3 What special role will Daria have?

2 Look at the handout for the students. Make sure you understand all the words. Do you think they will have to survive in a rainforest, a desert or at sea?

Name: _____

four bottles of water
a box of matches
a blanket
a penknife
a small mirror
a torch
a spade
a sleeping bag

3 ▶ 06 Watch the group doing the activity and answer the questions.

1 Where do they have to survive?
2 What five items do they choose?

4 Watch again and answer the questions.

1 How does Daria show from the start that she is leading the group?
2 Does she include everyone in the discussion?
3 Does anyone talk for too long?
4 Lulu interrupts politely once. What does she say?
5 In what way are the other interruptions not polite?

5 ▶ 07 Watch the students discussing their performance. Do they have the same answers to the questions in Exercise 4 as you?

6 What do you think? Did the group choose the most important items? Discuss in pairs.

7 Now work in groups of four and plan your own survival challenge. You will have to survive in a boat at sea.

- Choose a group leader.
- Decide what his/her role will be.
- Decide how you will reach decisions.

8 Read your survival challenge on page 127. You have 15 minutes to reach a decision.

9 Discuss how well your discussion went. Use this checklist.

- Did the group leader include everyone?
- Did you take turns?
- Did you interrupt politely?
- Did you reach an agreement?

SELF-ASSESSMENT: UNIT 8

How confident do you feel about:

- understanding the information in real-world notices?
- understanding opinions in an article?
- understanding the gist of short conversations?
- giving written advice, for example on a website?
- using the first conditional for talking about future possibilities?
- making sentences with *if*, *when* and *unless*?
- using words to describe weather and outdoor equipment?
- participating actively in discussions?

What was your favourite part of Unit 8? Tell your partner.

DIGITAL CLASSROOM
PERSONALISED LEARNING

VOCABULARY REFERENCE

WEATHER

1 Match the words to the photos. What is your (least) favourite type of weather? Why?

a breeze   a gale   a humid day   icy conditions   lightning
a shower   snowfall   sunshine   a (thunder)storm   a rainbow

OUTDOOR EQUIPMENT

DIGITAL CLASSROOM
PRACTICE EXTRA UNIT 8

2 Match the words to the photos.

first-aid kit   fishing rod   flask   helmet   hood   mosquito spray   penknife   torch
walking boots   waterproof clothes   Wellington boots (wellies)   wetsuit

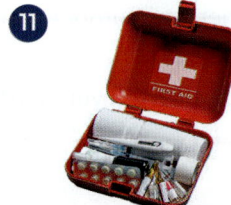

UNIT 9 A GREAT JOB

LEARNING AIMS

- **Skills:** discuss and create texts about jobs
- **Grammar:** learn and practise using relative clauses and making comparisons
- **Vocabulary:** learn and practise words and phrases for different jobs and the world of work
- **Critical thinking:** work together to imagine a job in the future
- **Exam practice:** Reading Parts 5 and 6, Listening Part 3

THE CHALLENGE

Jobs are changing and young people need new skills for their working life.

You will:

- **Stage 1 Think:** find out more about how jobs are changing.
- **Stage 2 Prepare:** focus on skills that will be important in the future.
- **Stage 3 Develop:** share information and plan a poster or presentation.
- **Stage 4 Present:** present ideas for learning these skills.

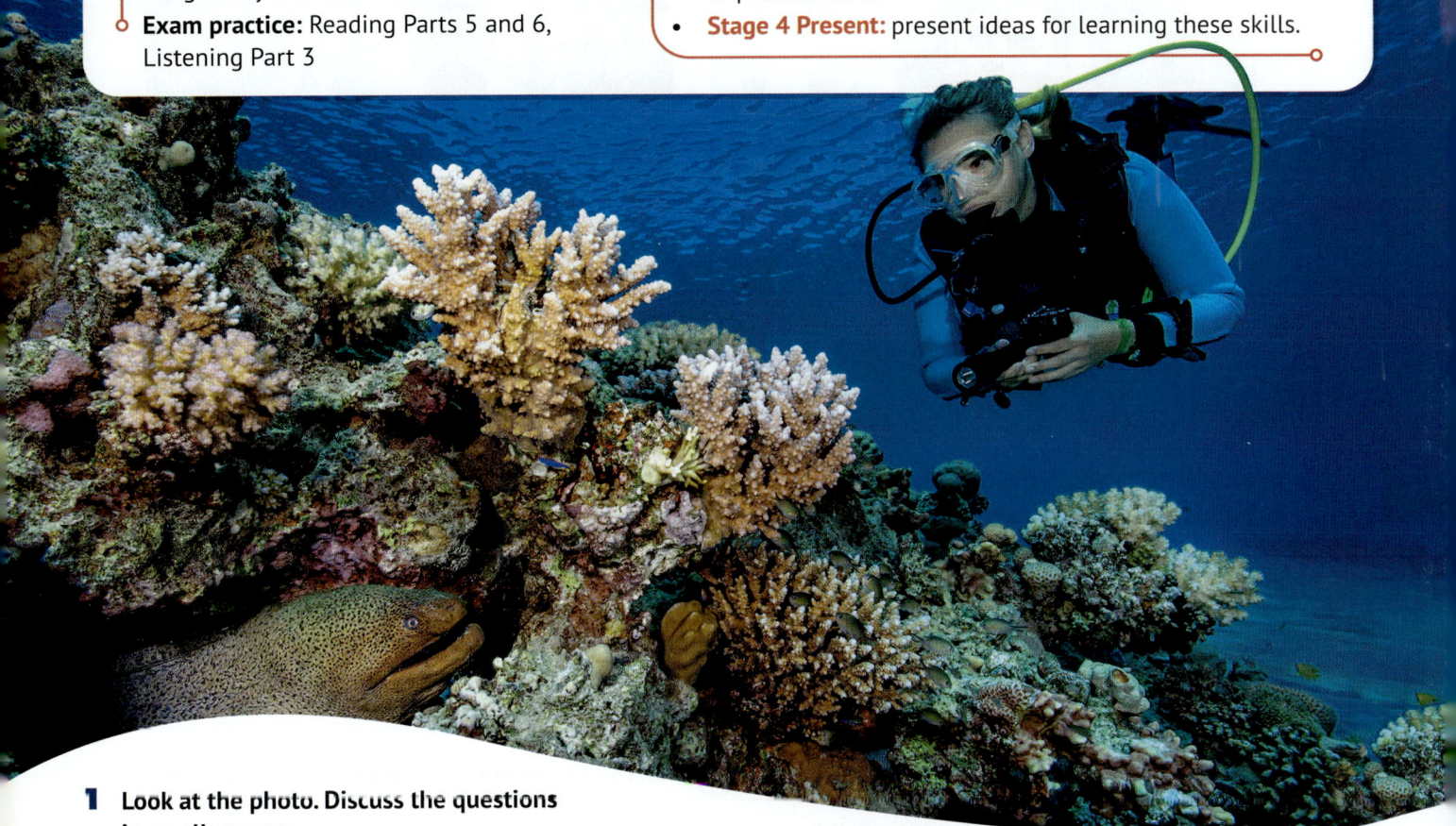

1 Look at the photo. Discuss the questions in small groups.

1 What is the boy's job?
2 Do you think the boy is happy at work? Why?
3 Do you think this is a job he will do for his whole life? Why? / Why not?

2 Watch the video and answer the questions.

1 Are most workers satisfied with their jobs?
2 What three types of worker are mentioned?
3 What factors are mentioned which can make people feel happy with their jobs?

CHALLENGE ①②③④

Think

Discuss the questions with a partner and make notes.

1 What jobs exist today which did not exist 50 years ago?
2 In what ways have people's working hours and workplaces changed?
3 Can you imagine any jobs that do not exist yet but will be needed in the future?

Documentary

Grammar

Grammar

VOCABULARY

JOBS

1 📱 🔊 **9.1 Go to the digital activity and match the words to the photos. Listen, check and repeat.**

architect   babysitter   baker   barber
designer   guard   journalist   judge
lawyer   programmer   scientist   travel agent

▶ **Vocabulary reference page 96**

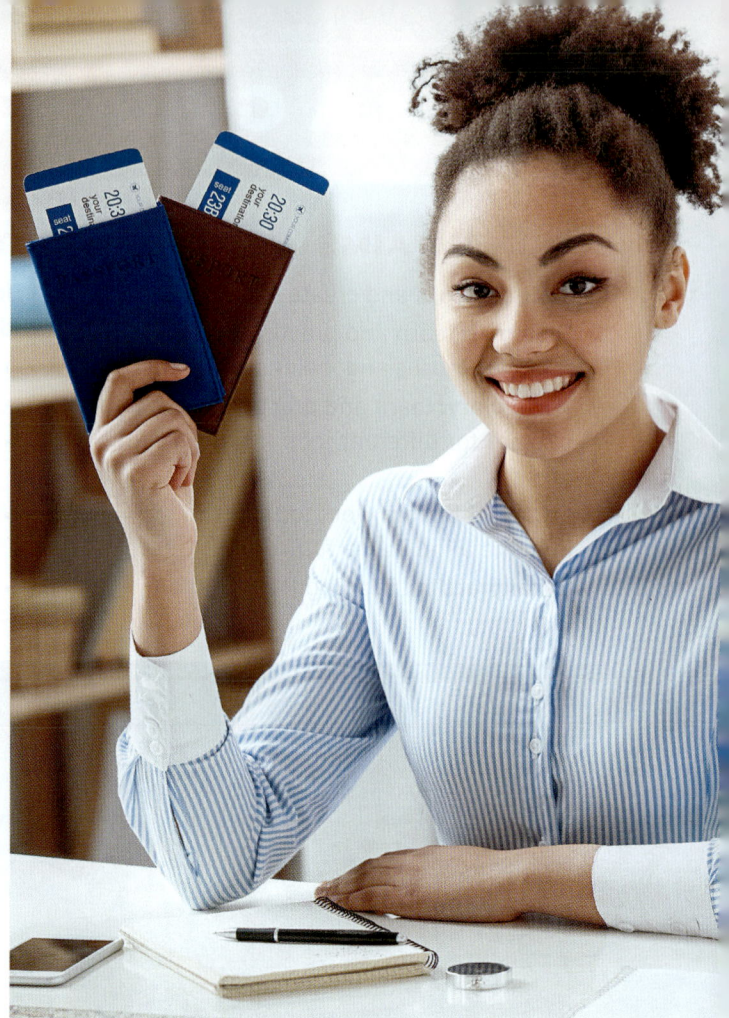

2 **Complete the sentences with the words in Exercise 1.**

1 A hairdresser for men is called a(n) _____.

2 A person who looks after children while their parents go out is a(n) _____.

3 This person makes important decisions in court: a(n) _____.

4 Someone who writes computer programs is a(n) _____.

5 If you don't want to plan your own holiday, you can go to a(n) _____.

6 Someone who plans how things (e.g. clothes) will look is a(n) _____.

7 Someone who plans buildings is a(n) _____.

8 This person makes bread and cakes: a(n) _____.

9 A person who writes articles for newspapers, magazines, etc. is a(n) _____.

10 If you need help with a legal problem, you can go to a(n) _____.

11 Someone who protects a place or people is a(n) _____.

12 A person who works in science is a(n) _____.

3 **Will people always think that the jobs in Exercise 1 are important? Work in pairs and complete a table with the jobs. Add some more jobs that you know.**

Needs a qualified person	A computer or robot could do it	I could do it myself at home

4 **Think back to the video and to the things that make people happy in their jobs. Which of the jobs in Exercise 1 do you think give people the highest job satisfaction? Why?**

>>> **STRETCH!** **Think of the people in your life who have jobs. Do you know what their jobs are called in English? If not, find out!**

🛡 CHALLENGE ─❶─❷─❸─❹

Prepare

1 Form groups of three people.

2 Look at your ideas about jobs that will be needed in the future.

3 Pick three different jobs which are realistic and important.

4 Each person will find out more about one of those jobs and the skills needed to do it.

5 Talk about where you could find information and then start your research.

READING

A SHORT TEXT

1 In some countries, secondary school students do work experience. Work in groups and discuss what you think this is, and whether you think it is a good idea.

2 Skim the text and choose the correct answer.

The writer lives in a small village. How were they able to take part in a useful work experience programme?

A They travelled to an office every day.

B They did it online.

C They did jobs in their house.

Work experience ... at home ◁) 9.2

It is difficult for people in my village to find a good job. We're far away from any city, so this is not a good ¹ ____ for big companies. Some people are farmers, and others travel a long ² ____ to get to work.

However, working from home is a new possibility. Companies now see that they can ³ ____ people who live quite far from the office, and some even offer virtual work experience programmes for students. I did one!

I worked for one week at an architects' office. I met the architects and found ⁴ ____ about the skills they need to do their jobs well. I took part in online meetings and had fun on virtual lunch ⁵ ____. I don't know if I really helped my 'colleagues', but I ⁶ ____ some of my ideas about buildings in the future, and they really listened. Now I'm sure I want to be an architect.

3 For each question, choose the correct answer.

1 A space	B location	C ground	D section
2 A length	B gap	C distance	D trip
3 A apply	B rent	C elect	D employ
4 A in	B out	C over	D by
5 A breaks	B stops	C pauses	D rests
6 A solved	B taught	C explained	D analysed

4 Have you ever done any kind of work experience, or do you know someone who has? Tell a partner.

>>> **STRETCH!** Go online and see if you can find work experience programmes. Are there any in your part of the world? Are there any for people your age?

ORACY

Showing interest

People will enjoy talking to you if you show interest in what they are saying. You should maintain eye contact and use positive body language. You can make comments such as 'That sounds like fun!', 'Really?' and 'Wow!'. You can also ask questions such as 'Why do you think that?'

5 Imagine you have a virtual work-experience week this term. Answer these questions and then tell a partner about your perfect work experience. Your partner should show interest in your idea. Then swap roles.

- What industry is it in?
- Is there one particular company that interests you?
- What do you want to learn about working in this company or industry?
- Who do you want to meet?

6 Did your partner show interest in your perfect work experience? If so, how?

GRAMMAR

RELATIVE CLAUSES

1 Watch the grammar animation. We see Sophie and Chris acting out two unusual jobs. What are they?

▶ 02

2 Choose the correct pronouns to complete the sentences. Then complete the grammar rules.

1 I want a job *which / who* is really fun.
2 I don't want a job *where / that* is boring.
3 People *who / which* love their job are really lucky.
4 I feel sorry for people *which / that* dislike their job.
5 We live in a village *that / where* it's hard to find a job.
6 There are some people *who / whose* job can be done at home.

Relative clauses

Relative clauses are introduced by relative pronouns (*that, which, where, who* and *whose*).
1 To add information about things, we can use _____ or _____.
2 To add information about people, we can use _____ or _____.
3 We use _____ to add information about places.
4 We use _____ with a noun to mean *his/her/their/its*.

▶ Grammar reference and practice page 122

3 🖥 Go to the digital activities.

4 Put the sentences together using relative clauses with *who* or *which*.

1 I know a man. The man is a professional musician.
2 It's a great job. The job makes him happy.
3 He plays music for people. The people are celebrating special events.
4 He also plays in a band. The band won an important music prize last year.
5 The band is looking for someone. The person can play the saxophone.
6 The saxophone is an instrument. It's not easy to play.

5 Complete the text with *which, that, who, whose* or *where*. If it is possible to leave out the relative pronoun, leave the gap empty.

A caretaker is person [1] _____ looks after a big building, like a school or a sports centre. It's a job [2] _____ you usually do alone, so it's not for everyone. Some caretakers work in places that are not very exciting, but what if you worked in a place [3] _____ everyone wants to go? You could work for someone [4] _____ property is amazing. What about being a caretaker on a private island? It's a job [5] _____ really exists! You have to do some work on the parts of the island [6] _____ people live. However, you also have lots of time to relax on the beach! So, have you got a friend [7] _____ has a private island? Can you tell me if there's someone [8] _____ you know? I'll work for them!

⟫⟫ **STRETCH!** Can we leave out the relative pronouns *whose* or *where*? Write some sentences with *whose* and *where*, and then decide what the rule is.

READING

A SHORT TEXT

☑ **EXAM TASK** READING PART 6

1 🔊 9.3 For each question, write the correct answer. Write one word for each gap.

👥 MEDIATION WORKSHEET

My sister Nola works at the zoo. There's a really big one in the city [1] _____ we live. Nola feeds the animals and keeps them clean. It sounds easy but she mustn't [2] _____ a mistake and give an animal the wrong food or let one escape. Nola's studying zoology so she hopes she'll have a(n) [3] _____ interesting job than this later, but for now she's happy. She enjoys talking to the people [4] _____ visit the zoo and have questions. Some animals need breakfast very early so Nola gets [5] _____ at 5 am, but she's a morning person, so that's OK.

It's a great job for a student, [6] _____ he or she doesn't like animals, but that's very unusual. Most young people love animals, I think.

HOW IS UNIT 9 SO FAR?

☆☆☆ I understand   ☆☆ I'm getting there   ☆ I don't understand

I DON'T WANT A 'REAL JOB'

THINK OUTSIDE THE BOX!

posted by: **Sunita_M** · 3 hours ago

Hi all! I'm looking for opinions today. As you know, I'm a successful blogger and a vlogger. I'm still at school, so I can't spend as much time on my vlogs as I want to, but a lot of people watch them.

Today at school, a careers adviser came to talk to us. I told her I wanted to be an influencer, and she said 'That's not a real job.' I thought that was very old-fashioned and asked her what she thought a real job was. These were her ideas: in a 'real job', you sign a contract with an employer. It could be a part-time or a full-time job but you should have a regular salary, which is what an employment contract gives you. It's a kind of security.

Sorry, but I don't want to be an employee. I want to be self-employed and make my own decisions. Influencers aren't lazy people. They work hard and pay taxes like other people. So why is being an influencer not a 'real job'?

I said all that to the careers adviser, and she said I was a good speaker and could make a career as a lawyer. A lawyer? Yes, that's a well-paid job and I suppose it could be interesting for many people, but I'm sure it's not for me.

So who is right? The careers adviser or me? Should I plan to become an employee in the future and forget my dreams of being an influencer? Please comment below!

READING

A BLOG POST

1 Which of these professions would you say are 'real jobs'? Work in pairs and discuss.

> customs officer   gamer   influencer   poet
> police officer   sailor   tour guide   vlogger

2 9.4 Read and listen to the blog post and answer the questions.

1   Why can't Sunita be a full-time vlogger now?
2   Why did Sunita think the careers adviser was 'old-fashioned'?
3   What does the careers adviser say about the money you earn as an employee?
4   What advantage of being self-employed does Sunita mention?
5   What does she think could be good about being a lawyer?

3 Now write a comment on Sunita's post. Write four to five sentences giving your opinion.

4 Critical Thinking   What do you think Sunita will really do in the future? Will she become a famous influencer, a lawyer or something else? Work in pairs and discuss.

VOCABULARY

THE WORLD OF WORK

1 9.5 Complete the collocations with the words. Listen, check and repeat.

> career   contract   employee   employer
> full-time   part-time   salary
> self-employed   taxes   well-paid

▶ **Vocabulary reference page 96**

1   a(n) ____, ____, ____ job
2   be a(n) ____, ____
3   be ____
4   earn a(n) ____
5   make a(n) ____
6   pay ____
7   sign a(n) ____

2   Go to the digital activity and talk about the people in the photos using the collocations in Exercise 1.

3   PRONUNCIATION   Go to the digital pronunciation activity.

4 Think of a job that you would really like. Make notes on the questions and then tell your partner about the job.

- What is the job?
- Is it part-time or full-time?
- Are you an employee or self-employed?
- What is good about the job?

>>> **STRETCH!** Find out about employment for young people in your country. What are the rules?

GRAMMAR

NON-DEFINING RELATIVE CLAUSES; COMPARISONS WITH (NOT) AS ... AS

1 Watch the grammar vlog. Alex has two work experience options. Does she choose one of them in the end?

▶ 03

2 Look at the examples from the grammar vlog and complete the grammar rules with *defining* or *non-defining*.

Defining relative clauses	Non-defining relative clauses
They produce films which are popular all over the world.	Option one is Sunrise Farm, which is a lovely place.
People who get a job there are really lucky.	The farm is also a hotel, which is why I'm interested in it.

Non-defining relative clauses

1 ____ relative clauses help us describe a person, a place or thing we are talking about.

2 ____ relative clauses give us extra information that does not affect the meaning of the sentence.

▶ Grammar reference and practice page 122

3 🖳 Go to the digital activities.

4 Work in pairs. Complete the sentences with your own ideas.

1 We like teachers who ...
2 Painting pictures is an unusual job, which ...
3 We love places where ...
4 We want friends whose ...

>>> STRETCH! Like *where*, some other question words can also be relative pronouns. Research examples of *when* and *why* used as relative pronouns.

5 Look at the sentences from the grammar vlog and complete the grammar rules and examples.

It's not as easy as it sounds.
Some people don't want to travel as far as they did in the past.

Comparisons with (not) as ... as

We can use (*not*) ____ ... ____ to compare things.

My father's job is ____ ____ well paid ____ my mother's job.

However, his job is ____ interesting ____ her job. They're both very interesting.

▶ Grammar reference and practice page 122

6 Rewrite the sentences using (*not*) *as ... as*. Do you think the sentences are true?

1 Working on a farm is harder than working in an office.
Working in an office is not as hard as working on a farm.

2 Teachers are happy and sales assistants are happy, too.

3 Working outside is more enjoyable than working inside.

4 Bankers are better paid than bakers.

DIGITAL CLASSROOM
PRACTICE EXTRA UNIT 9

ORACY

Justifying your ideas

When someone asks your opinion, you may immediately say what you think. It's also important to say *why* that's your opinion. People will take an opinion more seriously if there are reasons for it.

7 🔊 9.6 Listen to a girl talking about architects. How many reasons does she give for her opinion?

8 Work in pairs and compare the jobs. Which one is best in each pair?

- lawyer or judge
- police officer or guard
- hairdresser or barber
- programmer or journalist
- footballer or gamer

WRITING

A DESCRIPTION

1 Look at the photo and say what the woman's job is. Would you like to do this job in the future? Why? / Why not?

2 In one minute, write down all the words you can think of to describe personality, e.g. *patient, confident*, etc. Then share your words with your classmates. Decide together what kind of personality you think a kindergarten teacher needs.

3 A careers adviser has asked everyone in a class to write a description of their ideal job, and why they think they would be good at it. Read Marcel's text and answer the questions.

1 How has he shown that he can be a patient teacher?
2 How has he shown that he is confident?

My ideal job

I want to be a kindergarten teacher. Working with very young children is a lot of fun, and I think I would be good at it.

People who work with young children have to be patient. The teacher should give the children plenty of time to see what they can achieve. He or she mustn't get angry when they make mistakes. I am very patient. I recently taught my little niece how to write her name. It was very difficult for her, but she wanted to do it and now she can.

You also need to be confident for this job. As the captain of my local under-15s football team, I make quick, clear decisions. That is really important if you work with a group of children. If they think that you are unsure, they won't listen to you.

I'm confident and patient, and young children like me. That's why I think I would be an ideal kindergarten teacher.

4 The careers adviser is coming to your class, too. Write a description like Marcel's. Include:

- an introduction saying what job you want and why.
- two personal qualities people need for the job.
- examples of how you have shown both those personal qualities in your life.
- a short conclusion.

5 Read your description again and revise it. Use these questions to help you.

1 Have you included an introduction and a conclusion?
2 Have you named two personal qualities that are important for the job?
4 Have you showed examples of those qualities from your life?
5 Can you see any problems with the language (spelling, grammar, etc.)?

6 Now work in pairs. Read each other's descriptions and give feedback. Use the questions in Exercise 5 to help you. Make a note of your partner's feedback and write a second draft.

7 Read the model answer.

CHALLENGE — ① ② ③ ④

Develop

1 Pick one job to focus on.
2 Decide how you will present what you have learned, for example, on a poster or through a presentation.
3 Make notes on your information and ideas under these headings: *the job, qualities and skills needed for the job, how we could learn the skills*.
4 Create a first draft, for example of a poster or of notes for a presentation.

A MONOLOGUE

1 **What are your hobbies? Could any of them also be your job in the future? Tell a partner.**

2 **The person in the photo is an animator. Do you know what animators do? Discuss with a partner.**

✓ EXAM TASK LISTENING PART 3

EXAM TIP

When you check your answers, make sure that you have followed the instructions and not written too many words. You can only write one or two, and if you've written more than that, your answer will be incorrect.

3 🔊 **9.7 For each question, write the correct answer in the gap. Write one or two words or a number or a date or a time.**

You will hear a woman called Freya Bright telling a group of students about her work as an animator.

My job as an animator

As a child, Freya told stories with 1 _____ .

Freya studied 2 _____ at university.

Her degree course was quite 3 _____ for her.

She got the job she has now when she was 4 _____ .

She says people who work in companies must have good 5 _____ skills.

After work Freya sometimes plays 6 _____ .

ORACY

Ending a presentation

When you give a presentation, you don't just stop speaking at the end. You might ask if people have questions and before that, you should tell people that your speech is over. You can use quite formal phrases such as *So that brings me to the end of my presentation* or simpler, less formal ones, like *That's all. Thanks for listening.* It depends on who your audience is.

4 🔊 **9.8 Listen again to the end of Freya's speech and answer the questions in pairs.**

1 What phrase tells you that the presentation is over?

2 What does the phrase tell you about her relationship with her audience and how formal the situation is?

5 **Freya says 'For some people it's better if a hobby is *just* a hobby.' Can you remember why? Work in pairs and discuss.**

6 🛡️ **Critical Thinking Write some questions for Freya. Then work in pairs and ask and answer your questions. Take turns being Freya and the questioner.**

🛡️ CHALLENGE — 1 — 2 — 3 — 4

Present

1 Check that the information is clear in your first draft.

2 Practise explaining your poster / making your presentation.

3 Create a second draft.

4 Present your 'job of the future' to your classmates.

WRAP UP

Look back at the unit. Write down:

① some new vocabulary you learned to talk about jobs.

② your main role in the challenge.

③ five relative pronouns.

④ a sentence that compares two things with *as ... as*.

⑤ something in the unit that you especially enjoyed.

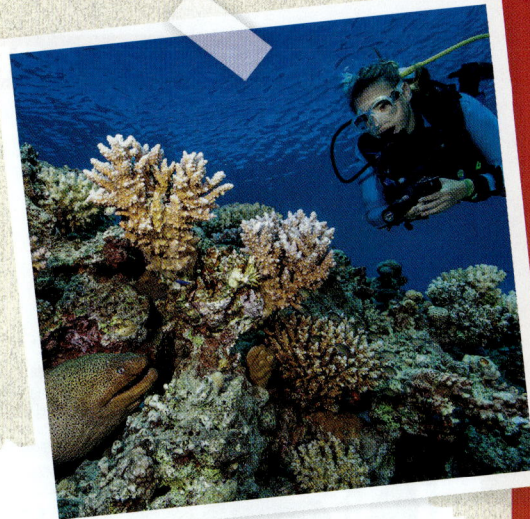

Sustainability

1 Look back at the reading on page 91. What do you really want to be in the future? Why?

2 How sustainable will your future job be?

SELF-ASSESSMENT: UNIT 9

How confident do you feel about:

- completing short texts with the best words?
- writing a description of a job that you would like?
- understanding detailed information in a monologue?
- talking about jobs and showing interest when a partner talks?
- using defining and non-defining relative clauses?
- making comparisons with *(not) as ... as*?
- naming and describing different jobs?
- imagining the world of work in the future?

What was your favourite part of Unit 9? Tell your partner.

Creative Thinking

1 Think about all the different activities your teacher has to do to teach a course.

2 Imagine you're a teacher for a week. What things make you feel happy? What things are you worried about? How do you feel about being a teacher? Talk to a partner.

>>> STRETCH! YOUR CHOICE

Now, choose an option.

Option 1:
Find out about a job that no longer exists and make a poster about it. Show what the job involved, why it was important in the past and why we no longer need people to do it.

Option 2:
Make a quiz for your classmates called 'What's the perfect job for you?' Write multiple-choice questions and then write what job would be good for people who chose 'mostly A / mostly B / mostly C'. Do the quiz with your classmates.

Option 3:
Go for a walk down one street and make a note of all the jobs you can think of that are done on that street. You might see some employees (e.g. shop assistants, bus drivers) but also ask yourself questions such as: *Who cleans the street? Who repairs the streetlamps? Who ...?*

VOCABULARY REFERENCE

JOBS

1 Match the jobs to the photos.

architect   babysitter   baker   barber   designer   guard   journalist
judge   lawyer   programmer   scientist   travel agent

THE WORLD OF WORK

DIGITAL CLASSROOM
PRACTICE EXTRA UNIT 9

2 Use the collocations to talk about the people and jobs in the photos.

a full-time job   a part-time job   a well-paid job   be an employee   be an employer
be self-employed   earn a salary   make a career   pay taxes   sign a contract

UNIT 10 DREAMS AND AMBITIONS

LEARNING AIMS

- **Skills:** discuss and create texts about dreams and ambitions
- **Grammar:** learn and practise the second conditional and third conditional
- **Vocabulary:** learn and practise adjectives of feeling and verb–noun collocations
- **Oracy:** participate in an interview
- **Exam practice:** Reading Part 3, Speaking Part 4, Writing Part 1

ORACY

Interviewing
- listening actively
- asking open questions
- asking follow-up questions

1 **Look at the photo. Discuss the questions in small groups.**

1 Why are the girls happy?
2 What might they be thinking right now?
3 Can you guess what they would like to achieve in the future?

2 **Watch the video and answer the questions.**

1 What is the 'American dream'?
2 How can one person's dream help other people?
3 What do you think of the dreams of the two famous people mentioned in the videos?

3 **Work in pairs. You are going to interview a person who has a big dream or ambition. Write down some questions you could ask.**

4 **Student A, you are someone with a big dream (you can choose someone you know, a celebrity or you can make up the information). Student B, interview this person about their dream. Then swap roles.**

5 **Think about your interview in Exercise 4. Did you use any of the skills in the Oracy box? Which ones? Compare your answers.**

Documentary

Grammar

Grammar

Oracy

VOCABULARY

ADJECTIVES OF FEELING

1 🖥 🔊 **10.1 Go to the digital activity and match the words to the photos. Listen, check and repeat.**

amazed / amazing   amused / amusing

annoyed / annoying   confused / confusing

disappointed / disappointing

embarrassed / embarrassing

frightened / frightening   relaxed / relaxing

▶ Vocabulary reference page 106

2 **Make two short sentences about each picture. Use a pair of adjectives from Exercise 1.**

The boy is amazed. He is looking at an amazing fish.

3 **Complete the conversation with adjectives from Exercise 1.**

What kind of career do you want? I want to do something ¹ _____, like going on missions to Mars.

Really? I find that idea ² _____ because it's so dangerous! I don't know what I want to do. I sometimes get ³ _____ by all the different job and career options that exist. I just want a normal job with lots of time off to take ⁴ _____ holidays.

Yes, holidays are important. Anyway, you're so clever, you can have any job!

Oh, stop! I don't like it when mum tells everyone I will one day be president. It's ⁵ _____ and always makes my face go red! Although, she was ⁶ _____ by my exam results because they weren't the best in the class.

My parents are very different. I get ⁷ _____ because they *don't* expect me to be the best. When I tell them my astronaut ambitions, they're ⁸ _____. Really, they laugh! But I'm going to show them that I can achieve anything I want!

4 **Work in pairs and think of examples of these things.**

an amazing sight   an amusing film

an annoying sound   a confusing situation

a disappointing day   an embarrassing situation

a frightening book   a relaxing activity

5 **Discuss how these things would make you feel. Use adjectives from Exercise 1.**

- You are watching a horror film.
- Your exam results are not very good.
- You are on a busy, lively and loud beach.

≫ STRETCH! Adjectives often end in *-ing* and *-ed*. Other common adjective endings are: *-ful*, *-able/-ible* and *-ic*. Write down some adjectives you can think of with these endings.

When I was younger, Ⓒ I wanted to be ... 🔊 10.2

Seventeen-year-old Salma Aboul writes about powerful dreams.

I've always wanted to be a journalist! But how can I make sure this childhood dream comes true? By being clear about my goal! If I want to work for an international newspaper, I need to focus on one area, possibly sport. Next, I should create an action plan with some 'easy to achieve' steps. I know I can do this. Just look at these three incredible people who are following their dreams!

READING

AN ARTICLE

1 Look at the photo and read the title of the article. What do you think it is about?

2 Read the article. Which of the people do you respect the most? Why?

EXAM TIP

Read each question carefully. Then find the information in the text which answers it. Underline the answer and write the question number next to it as this will make it easier for you to check your work at the end.

✓ EXAM TASK READING PART 3

3 For each question, choose the correct answer. Remember to find the relevant information first and write the question number next to it.

1 What is the purpose of Salma's article?
A to prevent other young people from being disappointed
B to encourage other young people to keep on trying
C to warn other young people against working for a newspaper
D to advise other young people on their future career

2 What does Salma say about Claire and her brother?
A Claire would be embarrassed to work with her brother.
B Claire's brother taught her not to be afraid of anything.
C Claire has the greatest respect for her brother.
D Claire's brother was annoyed when Claire got the job.

3 We learn from the text that Salma is
A amused that Luna wanted to help insects.
B confused that Luna had to pay to study.
C annoyed that Luna was the only student to help animals.
D amazed that Luna could pay her own rent.

4 Salma dreams that Omar will
A win an important competition.
B take up more sports.
C learn to compete alone.
D become a member of the local team.

5 What would Salma say to a friend?

A It's a shame about Claire. She regrets spending so much time at the fire station and not hanging out with her friends.

B It was stupid not to follow my childhood dream. Like most other people, I decided to do something different.

C Luna was born to be a vet and she did everything she could to achieve her goal. Nothing could ever stop her!

D Although Omar is a talented athlete, I would be surprised if he took up other sports.

4 Now go back and check your choice for each answer carefully against the text.

5 Salma would like to include another person in her article. Who would you include? Why? What would you say about them?

BLOGS ˅   NEWSLETTERS ˅   VIDEOS ˅

From an early age, Claire used to visit her local fire station. The large fire trucks, heavy equipment and loud noises scared her, but her big brother was working there. She wanted to grow up to be like him! At school, she made sure she passed everything with good grades. She had listened to her brother and knew it would be useful to learn sign language, too. As soon as she was old enough, she applied to work there. Nobody was surprised when she was offered a job. Now Claire is a firefighter who can think clearly in an emergency, and she doesn't find the station frightening anymore.

Luna was one of many children who dreamed of being a vet. She was the typical child who used to open the window to let flies out, rescue birds and other small animals and take them to the local animal centre. In other words, if Luna was able to save an animal, she would! She lived in a small apartment with her mum and grandma and they couldn't afford to keep a pet. Luna was creative and began to offer a dog-walking service so she could spend time with animals. After several years, she had not only saved enough money for the fees for vet school, but she also had some left for her accommodation, too.

Omar is an amazing athlete with huge ambitions. Omar was born with cerebral palsy. He has difficulty in moving and keeping his balance so he gets around in a wheelchair. However, with the help of his three-wheeled frame runner, Omar can take part in sports competitions on his own. If Omar continues to break records, he may be asked to join the national team. And if that happened, he could become an Olympic champion.

GRAMMAR

SECOND CONDITIONAL

1 Watch the video. Would Alex like to change anything about himself? Why? / Why not?

▶ 02

2 Choose the correct words to complete the grammar rules.

> **Second conditional**
>
> **1** We use the second conditional to talk about *likely / unlikely* situations. We can use it to talk about the *past or present / present or future*.
>
> **2** We form the second conditional with *If + past simple / present simple, had / would* + infinitive. *If I had a lot of money, I'd buy a faster computer for gaming.*
>
> **3** When we *talk about future plans / give advice*, we often say, *If I was (or were) you, I'd … .*
>
> ▶ Grammar reference and practice page 123

3 🖥 Go to the digital activities.

4 🎨 Creative Thinking Work in pairs and read the situations. What would you do? Try to imagine at least two alternatives and possibilities for each situation.

1 You'd like to appear on TV but don't know how.
2 Your bedroom looks rather dull but you don't have much money to spend on it.
3 Your sports team is at the bottom of the league.
4 You've been offered a superpower of your choice. Which one would you choose?

>>> STRETCH! Choose two of the situations in Exercise 4 and find out what members of your family would do. Report back to the class.

SPEAKING

DISCUSSING LIKES, DISLIKES, EXPERIENCES, OPINIONS AND HABITS

1 🔊 10.3 Listen to an examiner talking to two candidates. Complete her questions.

1 Would you like to _____?
2 Do you prefer to _____ or _____?
3 Do you think it's important to _____?

2 What three questions does the examiner use to encourage the other candidate to speak?

> ☑ **EXAM TASK** SPEAKING PART 4
>
> **EXAM TIP**
>
> Listen carefully to the examiner's question, even if the question is for the other candidate. The examiner may ask you for your opinion immediately afterwards.
>
> **3** Work in groups of three. Take turns to be the examiner and one of the candidates. The examiner asks a question from Exercise 1. Then, the examiner asks the second candidate a prompt question from Exercise 2.

> **ORACY**
>
> **Listening actively**
>
> It's always important to show that you are listening, not just in an exam. Show interest in questions and react to exactly what was asked.

4 🔊 10.4 Now listen to Ela asking Matt the questions in Exercise 1. What phrases do they use to show they are listening?

> Difficult / Not an easy question!
> Go on, I'm listening.   Really?   Tell me more.
> That's a brilliant/good/great question!
> That's funny/interesting/amazing!   Yeah!
> You're joking / kidding / not serious!

5 Now work with a different partner. Ask and answer the questions in Exercise 1 again. This time, use the phrases in Exercise 4 to show you are listening.

HOW IS UNIT 10 SO FAR?

☆☆☆ I understand   ☆☆ I'm getting there   ☆ I don't understand

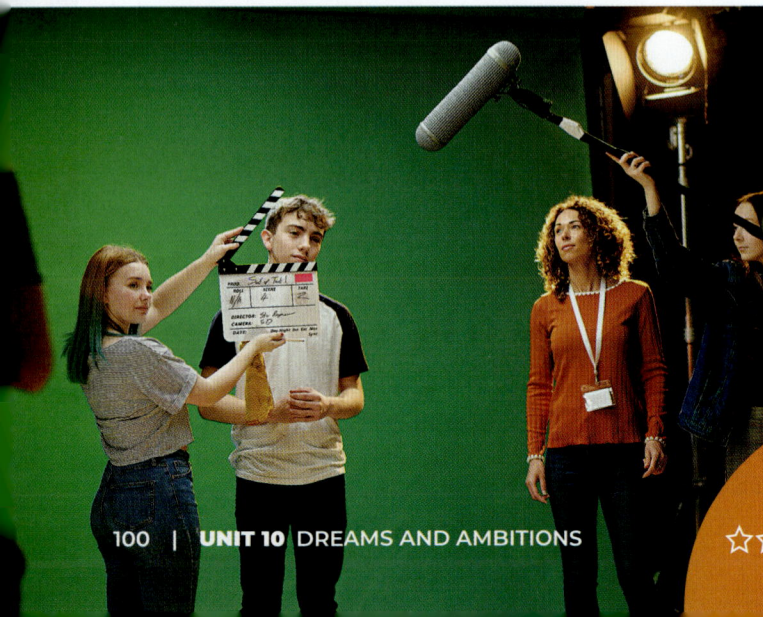

LISTENING

AN INTERVIEW

1 What do you think a *life coach* does? Work in pairs and discuss.

2 ◁)) **10.5** Now listen to an interview with a life coach. Which of these topics does she talk about?

- A how to do better at school
- B how to have a successful career
- C how to feel happier with yourself
- D how to find good friends

3 ◁)) **10.5** Listen again and complete the summary with words from the interview.

Carola does not think it is wrong to dream ¹ _____, but she does not want people to feel bad if they have a ² _____ life. She says achievement can feel ³ _____, but it's not the most important thing in life. She believes friends and hobbies can make you happy, and for some people it's a ⁴ _____. Carola thinks the most important thing is to live in the ⁵ _____. Enjoy what you do and remember that you don't have to be ⁶ _____.

ORACY

Asking open questions

If you ask questions that people can answer with *yes/no*, you may not get very long answers. Good interviewers ask open questions with *what, how, why,* etc.

4 Imagine a parent or other adult is asking you these questions. Which questions will get the longest answers from you?

1 Did you have a good day at school?
2 How was your day at school?
3 What subjects did you have today?
4 What did you do in maths/geography/history?

5 ◁)) **10.5** Carola's interviewer asks open questions. Complete the questions. Listen again and check.

1 Carola, _____ dreaming big?
2 _____ could come true in real life?
3 But we love our crazy dreams. _____ use their imagination?
4 No? Then _____?
5 Live in the moment. _____?

THINK OUTSIDE THE BOX!

6 🟢 **Critical Thinking** What do you think? Is Carola's advice good, or should young people be advised to focus on big dreams and achievement?

VOCABULARY

VERB–NOUN COLLOCATIONS

1 ◁)) **10.6** Make collocations with the verbs and nouns. Listen, check and repeat.

achieve your	an effort /	follow your	an ambition
give yourself	progress	have	dreams
make	goals	set yourself	imagination
see	results	use your	targets
	rewards		

2 🖥 Work in pairs. Go to the digital activity and talk about what the people are doing in the photos. Use the verb–noun collocations from Exercise 1.

▶ Vocabulary reference page 106

3 Complete the conversation with the collocations in Exercise 1. You may need to change the pronouns.

Interviewer: Riku, you've just won the City Speed Skating Championship. Congratulations! How did you achieve ¹ _____?

Riku: Thanks! It wasn't easy but I set ² _____ and I gave ³ _____ when I achieved them. I trained every day. You have to train hard if you really want to see ⁴ _____. A lot of people go inline skating every day, but just for fun. They become good at it but then they don't really make more ⁵ _____. That's OK if you don't have ⁶ _____ to be an Olympic roller speed skater, but that's my dream!

Interviewer: Wow! So, will you have to train even more?

Riku: Yes, I'll have to train more and I'll also have to use ⁷ _____ and think of new ways to get fitter and stronger. I'll have to make ⁸ _____ if I want to be better than I am now, but that's OK because it's really fun!

Interviewer: Well done for having the courage to follow ⁹ _____!

⟫⟫ STRETCH! Think back to the person you chose to include in Salma's article in Exercise 5 on pages 98–99. How did the person achieve their goal? Write a short report. You can use Salma's text as a model.

GRAMMAR

THIRD CONDITIONAL

1 Look at the pictures. Do you know who the people are? Watch the grammar animation and find out. ▶ 03

2 Look at the sentence from the grammar animation and complete the grammar rules with the words.

If we had been poor children back then, we would have worked hard in factories.

> past   past participle   past perfect

Third conditional

1 To make the third conditional, we use *if* plus the _____ in one clause and *would have* plus the _____ in the other clause.

2 We use the third conditional to talk about unreal situations in the _____.

▶ Grammar reference and practice page 123

3 📱 Go to the digital activities.

4 Choose the correct words to complete the text.

My childhood dream has come true: I'm a racing driver! If my dad [1] *hadn't given / wouldn't have given* me toy cars for my birthday, I [2] *hadn't had / wouldn't have had* the idea. I played with them all the time. When I got a bike, I always cycled too fast. My mum [3] *had been / would have been* happier if I [4] *had cycled / would have cycled* more slowly, but I love going fast. She wanted me to be a teacher. I [5] *hadn't been / wouldn't have been* happy if I [6] *had done / would have done* that. I know my job is dangerous, but I love it!

5 📱 PRONUNCIATION Go to the digital pronunciation activity.

6 Complete the text with the correct third conditional form of the verbs in brackets.

My dream has come true: we've got a cat! I've always wanted one, but my dad wasn't so sure. If he [1] _____ (make) the decision, we [2] _____ (get) a hamster! Luckily, my mum and my brothers wanted a cat, too. They [3] _____ (be) disappointed if we [4] _____ (buy) a hamster. We didn't actually buy the cat. My aunt's cat had kittens, so she gave us one. If that [5] _____ (not happen), we probably [6] _____ (not think) of getting a cat at the moment. But now we have him and I'm so happy! My aunt named him Tiger. I [7] _____ (not give) him that name if she [8] _____ (ask) me. He's black! Have you ever seen a black tiger?

7 Read about what these people did in strange situations. What would you have done in the same situation? Work in pairs and discuss.

- Marco met a bear in the forest. He ran away as fast as he could.
- Lucy's friend invited her to a party, but she didn't want to go. Lucy messaged her friend on the night of the party to say she was sick.
- Mani's aunt gave him a sweater that he didn't like. He said, 'Thank you, I love it.' But he never wore it.
- A shopkeeper gave Helena the wrong change when she bought some sweets. Helena left the shop and didn't say anything.

>>> STRETCH! Instead of *would have*, we can use *might have* and *could have* in a third conditional sentence. Do some research online and write some sentences of your own.

DIGITAL CLASSROOM ▶
PRACTICE EXTRA UNIT 10

WRITING

AN EMAIL

1 Read this email from an English friend and the notes. How would you answer Sam's questions?

> **< Inbox**   3 Messages   ∧ ∨
>
> Hi,
>
> I love your video channel. I've always dreamed of creating my own but I'm not sure how to start. ——————— **Amazing!**
>
> I was thinking of either posting tips for gamers or perhaps weekly reviews of new games. Which do you think would be more popular? ——— **Suggest and say why.**
>
> What's the best way to film the videos? Do I need any special equipment? ———————— **Explain.**
>
> And have you got any other useful advice?
>
> Let me know what you think!
>
> Sam

2 Now read this email. Does it answer all Sam's questions in Exercise 1? How is the information organised?

> **< Inbox**   2 Messages   ∧ ∨
>
> Hi Sam,
>
> Lovely to hear from you. I think it's cool that you're going to start your own channel for gamers. It'll be a success, I'm sure! Instead of choosing one idea, <u>if I were you, I'd create something more general</u>, for example, 'Weekly News for Gamers' so that it attracts more viewers.
>
> Filming yourself is embarrassing at first but then it gets easier! <u>I wouldn't buy new equipment for now because</u> the camera and microphone on your phone will be good enough. A friend once told me to make short videos first, film them once and try not to spend too much time editing them. <u>This advice has worked for me</u>!
>
> I can't wait to see your first videos!
>
> Beth
>
> **👥 MEDIATION WORKSHEET**

3 Look at the <u>underlined</u> expressions in the email in Exercise 2 and the phrases below. Do we use them to suggest, explain or tell something?

> For that reason, I would …   It's amazing!
> How/What about …?   Why don't you …?
> One of the best things to do is … as …
> There's so much you can do.

☑ EXAM TASK   **WRITING PART 1**

EXAM TIP

> Try to write around 100 words. If you write less, you may have left out some important information. If you write a lot more, then some of the information may not be relevant.

4 Read this email from an English friend and the notes you have made. Write your email to Ezra using all the notes.

> **< Inbox**   1 Message   ∧ ∨
>
> Hi,
>
> Congratulations on your award! I've always dreamed of winning a prize but I'm not sure what for! —— **Amazing!**
>
> Perhaps I should take up photography like you! Or should I look for something different? ——— **Suggest and say why.**
>
> What's the best way to learn how to do something well? Do I need to find a class? ——— **Explain.**
>
> And have you got any other useful advice? —— **Tell Ezra.**
>
> Let me know what you think!
>
> Ezra

5 Read your email again and revise your work. Use these questions to help you.

1 Does the email answer all four points in the notes? Is it well organised?
2 Does the email open and close properly?
3 Does it include expressions in Exercise 4?

6 Now work in pairs. Read each other's emails and give feedback. Use the questions in Exercise 5. Make notes and write a second draft.

7 🖳 Read the model answer.

LISTENING

SHORT MONOLOGUES

1 Work in pairs and answer the questions.

1 How often do you watch reality shows?
2 Why do people enjoy watching them?
3 Why do people enjoy taking part in them?

2 🔊 **10.7** Listen to three young people talking about reality shows. Match them to their feeling about the show (a–e). There are two extra feelings.

1	Lise	a	disappointed
2	Jakub	b	amused
3	Zeynep	c	frightened
		d	embarrassed
		e	annoyed

3 🔊 **10.7** Now listen again. Match the young people (1–3) with what they say (a–e). There are two extra sentences.

1 Lise   a I know someone who follows their dreams.
2 Jakub   b I'd love to appear on this show.
3 Zeynep   c I didn't like the way the programme ended.
           d I have an ambition to become great at something.
           e It's not always easy to watch my favourite programme when it's on.

4 If you could appear on any reality show, what would it be? Why? Use your imagination: you can make up a show!

ORACY

Asking follow-up questions

For a lively discussion, listen to what people say and react with follow-up questions, like 'Why do you say …?', 'What was that like?', etc.

5 🔊 **10.8** Listen to this extract from an interview. Which of the three questions you hear is a follow-up question?

ORACY

INTERVIEWING

- listening actively
- asking open questions
- asking follow-up questions

1 If you could be any person in history, who would you be? Why? Work in pairs and discuss.

2 Watch some students planning an interview with a historical figure. Answer the questions.

 ▶ 04

1 What person from history will they interview?
2 How will the interviewee prepare for the interview?
3 How will the others prepare?
4 What problem do they think they might have?

3 ▶ 04 Work in pairs. Watch the video again and check your answers.

4 ▶ 05 Now watch a video of the students doing the interview. Find at least one example of each of these things.

1 Danny showing that he is listening actively to the interviewers' questions
2 open questions
3 follow-up questions

5 ▶ 06 Watch the group discussing the interview and answer the questions.

1 Did the interviewee find his role hard? Why? / Why not?
2 Were the interviewers happy with their questions? Why? / Why not?
3 What would they do differently the next time?

6 Work in groups of four or five and plan an interview with a historical figure.

- Decide which of you will play the famous person.
- Decide who the famous person from history will be.
- Let the interviewee do some research about the person.
- Plan and write down some questions (but be ready to react spontaneously with follow-up questions).

7 Hold the interview. When you have finished, discuss how well your interview went. Use this checklist.

- Did the interviewee listen actively and answer the questions that were asked?
- Did the interviewers ask open questions which elicited good answers?
- Did the interviewers listen to the answers and respond with follow-up questions?

8 Did you find out anything about the famous person that you didn't know before? Do some research and find out more about one interesting point or event in the person's life. Tell your classmates what you have learned.

SELF-ASSESSMENT: UNIT 10

How confident do you feel about:

- reading a longer article for gist and for detail?
- understanding a radio or podcast interview?
- understanding short monologues about people's feelings?
- giving advice in an email?
- using the second and third conditionals?
- using collocations about dreams and ambitions?
- using adjectives to describe feelings?
- asking and answering questions in an interview?

What was your favourite part of Unit 10? Tell your partner.

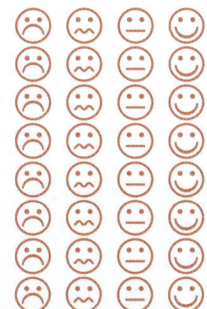

DIGITAL CLASSROOM
PERSONALISED LEARNING

VOCABULARY REFERENCE

ADJECTIVES OF FEELING

1 Match each pair of adjectives to a photo.

amazed / amazing   amused / amusing   annoyed / annoying   confused / confusing

disappointed / disappointing   embarrassed / embarrassing   frightened / frightening   relaxed / relaxing

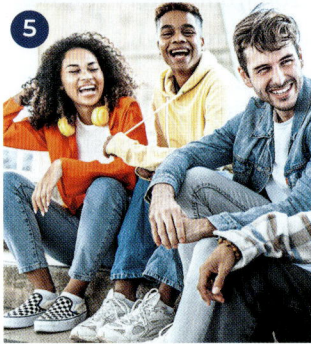

VERB–NOUN COLLOCATIONS

DIGITAL CLASSROOM
PRACTICE EXTRA UNIT 10

2 Use the collocations to describe what is happening in the photos.

achieve your goals   follow your dreams   give yourself rewards   have an ambition

make an effort   make progress   see results   set yourself targets   use your imagination

CONTENTS

GRAMMAR REFERENCE AND PRACTICE

STEAM INVESTIGATIONS

SCIENCE AND ENGINEERING

Does skateboarding defy the laws of physics?

HOW DO SKATEBOARDS WORK?

Competitive skateboarders can do a range of tricks. These require a well-designed board and an understanding of physics.

One trick is the Ollie, which requires the skateboarder to jump with the board. This happens in four steps:

① THINK

- Look at the photo. What is the skateboarder trying to do?
- What do you think will happen next in the photo?
- Which characteristics does a skateboard need to have?

The skateboarder crouches down on the board, when either **stationary** or moving along at constant velocity.

The skateboarder jumps upwards, pushing down with their back foot much harder than their front foot. This means that the back of the skateboard hits the ground very hard, which leads to a large upward **force** on the back of the board, causing it to move upwards.

④ INVESTIGATE: Which sports equipment should I buy?

🔍 RESEARCH

1.1 Consider the sports you enjoy playing. Make a list of the equipment needed for each sport.

1.2 Choose one sport and piece of equipment to investigate. Make a spidergram of the properties that are needed for the equipment to work.

1.3 Research different options for materials for your piece of equipment and what the pros and cons of each are.

✏️ CREATE

2.1 Using the information you have collected, design your ideal piece of equipment.

2.2 Think about what colours or patterns you want to use to make it visually appealing.

2.3 Make an advertising poster for your piece of equipment, remembering to make sure you've pointed out each material and why it is used, to encourage people to buy it.

The skateboarder uses their front foot to bring the board level in the air.

Gravity causes the board and skateboarder to fall back down to the ground, and the skateboarder lands the board.

For this trick, the skateboard needs a number of properties: to be stiff enough to exert a high force on the ground, yet **flexible** enough not to break when it experiences this force; to have low-**friction** wheels so the skateboard doesn't stop too quickly; to be made from a material that can be **moulded** into the correct shape; and to have a **rough** or high-friction surface, to allow good grip between the board and the skateboarder's feet.

③ EXPLORE

Match the sentence fragments to make complete sentences.

1. A skateboard needs to be flexible ____	a.	it hits the ground and an upward force is generated.
2. When the skateboarder pushes down on the back of the board ____	b.	causes the skateboard to move back towards the ground.
3. The surface of a skateboard is often rough ____	c.	so it does not break when large forces are placed upon it.
4. Gravity ____	d.	to allow them to jump up with a large force.
5. The skateboarder starts crouched down ____	e.	to allow good grip.

Draw a skateboard and label it with the properties mentioned in the text that are needed to perform tricks.

Glossary

flexible (adj) able to bend without breaking

force (n) influence that changes how an object is moving

friction (n) force that makes it hard for one object to move over another

gravity (n) force that makes things fall to the ground

mould (v) to make something have a particular shape

rough (adj) opposite of smooth

stationary (adj) not moving or changing

📽 PRESENT

3.1 Make a list of the important characteristics of your piece of equipment.

3.2 Think of possible questions your classmates may ask and how to answer those questions.

3.3 Present your advertising poster to the class. Convince the class of the advantages of your equipment.

3.4 Answer any questions your classmates may have about your piece of equipment.

💬 REFLECT

4.1 Consider the questions and feedback you have received. How could you improve your poster or your selling points further?

4.2 Which other piece of equipment did you find convincing?

STEAM INVESTIGATIONS

SCIENCE

How do animals adapt to their environment?

How do animals SURVIVE?

Animals adapt to the habitat they live in to survive. These **adaptations** may help with:

- **camouflage**.
- accessing food and water.
- surviving temperature changes.
- **deterring** or damaging **predators**.

For example, predators' eyes face forwards, giving them three-dimensional vision, helping them catch other animals. **Prey** often have their eyes to the sides of their heads, giving them a wider field of vision, reducing the chances of being caught.

① THINK

- What animals can you see in the photos?
- What's special about them?
- What animals live in your local environment? Why?

WOOD FROGS

Habitat: Woodland and swamps

Survival: Wood frogs build up high levels of sugar in their cells. This allows the cells to cool way down, with around 60% of their body freezing without damaging them. Their **core functions** also slow or stop. When the weather warms up, the frog unfreezes and carries on with life.

Camouflage and protection:

Coloured to fit in with leaf litter. They give off smelly chemicals to deter predators.

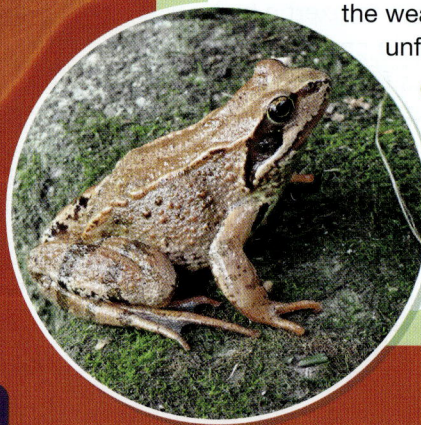

④ INVESTIGATE: How do animals adapt to their habitat?

🔍 RESEARCH

1.1 Choose two of the following habitats: rainforest, tundra, desert, polar ice, ocean, savannah, grasslands, mountain or coniferous forest.

1.2 Investigate the animals that live in your chosen habitats. In pairs, choose one from each to investigate further.

1.3 Research the animals you have chosen and how they are adapted to their habitats.

✏️ CREATE

2.1 Write a script for a podcast about your chosen habitats and animals, explaining how the animals have adapted to their environments.

2.2 Rehearse the script within your pair. Think about how you use your voice to engage your listener.

2.3 Record your podcast.

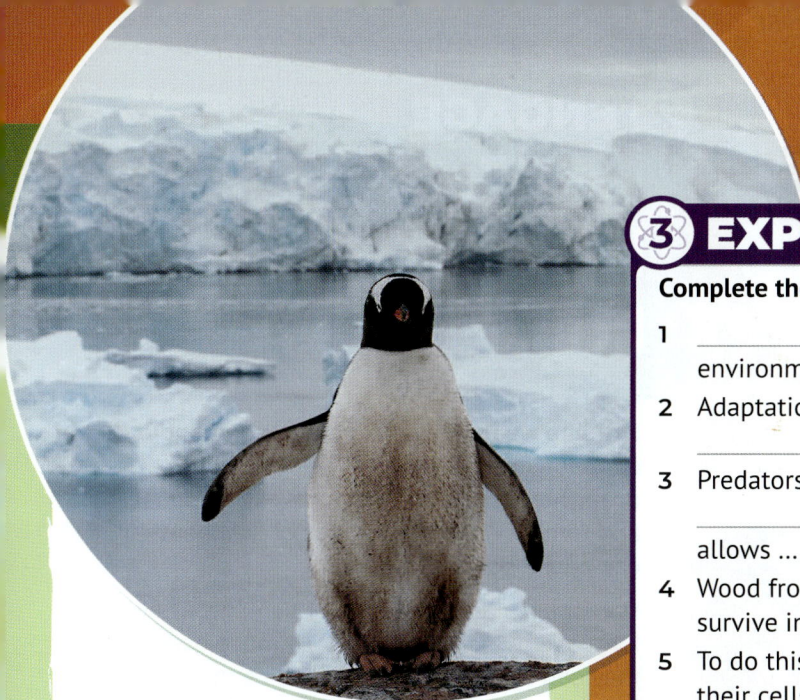

PENGUINS

Habitat: Land and at sea

Survival: Penguins can slow their heart rate when diving for a long period of time and speed it up when they resurface. They also reduce blood flow to their **peripheries**.

Penguins can get rid of salt very efficiently. This means they can drink sea water.

Camouflage and protection:

When swimming, their black backs make them blend in with the dark sea from above and their white tummies help them blend in with the bright background when being viewed from below.

③ EXPLORE

Complete the sentences using the information in the text.

1 _____ are important to help animals survive in their environment.
2 Adaptations can help animals stay _____, obtain _____ and water and _____ predators.
3 Predators have eyes on the _____ of their heads whilst _____ often have them to the side. This difference allows ....
4 Wood frogs have a specific adaptation to enable them to survive in very _____ temperatures.
5 To do this, they increase the amount of _____ in their cells.
6 Penguins are adapted to swim and dive. They have _____ backs and _____ tummies to help them blend into their environment.

Decide if the sentences refer to wood frogs or penguins, using the information in the fact cards.

1 They can bring their temperature down when it's cold outside.
2 They can drink salty water.
3 They can slow their hearts when diving.
4 They can stop their basic body functions.
5 Predators are scared away because of their smell.
6 They become invisible when seen from above or below in water.

Glossary

camouflage (n) the way that the colour or shape of an animal mixes with its natural environment

core functions (n) bodily functions needed for life, e.g. heart and brain functions

deter (v) to prevent something from happening

peripheries (n) the outer parts

predator (n) an animal that hunts, kills and eats other animals

prey (n) an animal which is hunted and killed for food

PRESENT

3.1 Decide how you will introduce your podcast to the class.

3.2 Introduce your podcast, making sure you use positive body language.

3.3 Provide constructive feedback to the other groups.

REFLECT

4.1 Write two things that are really good and one thing to improve in your podcast.

4.2 Compare your feedback to your own analysis.

4.3 Which animal did you find most interesting? Why?

STEAM INVESTIGATIONS

SCIENCE

What is the impact of extreme weather?

What's the difference?
Hurricanes and tornadoes

Extreme weather events have become more common in recent years. These include **droughts**, **floods** and heat waves. Hurricanes and tornadoes are both types of weather that can cause damage and injury.

Hurricanes can cause a lot of damage. They form over water, but when they move over land, they can cause **tidal surges** where the sea level can rise by up to 10 metres. This surge can destroy coastal towns due to the power of the water. Hurricanes also move large quantities of sand, and the winds can lead to **destruction** of property and trees. Low-lying areas are often flooded. There is a significant risk to life.

Tornadoes are smaller, faster and last for a shorter time. Some similarities and differences between hurricanes and tornadoes are shown on the opposite page.

① THINK

- What forms of weather have you heard of?
- Why do we need these different types of weather?
- These forms of weather can become extreme. What effects might these then have?

④ INVESTIGATE: Are models useful for understanding weather?

🔍 RESEARCH

1.1 Working in pairs, decide on a type of weather you are interested in, e.g. tornado, rain or snow.

1.2 Research a way in which you could model this phenomenon and gather everything you need to make your model.

1.3 Research your chosen weather and think about how the model can help you explain it.

✏️ CREATE

2.1 Create your model for your type of weather.

2.2 Make a table showing the strengths and limitations of the model in understanding the weather phenomenon.

2.3 Write a script explaining the type of weather, using your model to support your explanation. Point out the strengths and limitations of the model.

Scientists use information from satellites to study the size and direction of a hurricane. They use computer modelling to **predict** where tornadoes will form and hurricanes will move next and therefore, which communities need to prepare or **evacuate**. As the hurricane or tornado moves, they adapt their model.

	Hurricane	Tornado
How big are they?	up to several hundred kilometres wide	up to a few hundred metres wide
Where do they form?	over water	over land
How long do they last?	up to three weeks	up to about an hour
Wind speed?	generally below 330 km/h	up to 480 km/h
Wind movement?	a circular pattern	a circular pattern
Occurrence	around 10 per year starting in the Atlantic Ocean	800–1000 per year in the USA
Predictability	often possible to predict days in advance	generally, very difficult to predict in advance

③ **EXPLORE**

List the five types of extreme weather in the text.

Make a Venn diagram showing ways in which hurricanes and tornadoes are the same and how they are different.

Glossary

destruction (n) the act of damaging something so badly that it cannot be used

drought (n) a long period where there is little or no rain

evacuate (v) to move people from a dangerous place to somewhere safe

flood (n) a large amount of water covering an area which is usually dry

predict (v) to say an event or action will happen in the future

tidal surge (n) a sudden or great increase in the sea level

PRESENT

3.1 In small groups, demonstrate your model in action.

3.2 Present your script to the rest of your group, making sure that everyone has a chance to present.

3.3 Ask for and answer questions from the rest of your group.

REFLECT

4.1 Do you think that your model helped others understand your weather phenomenon?

4.2 How confident were you in thinking about the strengths and limitations of your model? Were you able to present these clearly?

4.3 How could you improve your model? What would you do differently?

GRAMMAR REFERENCE AND PRACTICE

PRESENT SIMPLE

We use the present simple:

- to talk about something we do regularly or things that usually happen.
  *Most evenings, we **play** video games after dinner.*
- for facts and things which are generally true and permanent.
  *My brother **doesn't live** near us.*
- for state verbs (what we like, think and feel). These are not normally used in continuous form.
  believe, dislike, hate, hope, know, like, love, prefer, remember, think, understand, want, wish

PRESENT CONTINUOUS

We use the present continuous:

- to talk about things that are happening now.
  *We're **sitting** on the train to London.* (= now)
- for things that are temporary.
  *I'**m practising** every day for the music exam next week.* (= only at the moment)

1 **Choose the correct form of the verbs to complete the sentences.**

1 My brother *runs / is running* for the school bus every morning because he *doesn't wake up / isn't waking up* on time.

2 *Do you believe / Are you believing* all the stories in the news?

3 *I have / I'm having* my break now. Our teacher *always gives / is always giving* us a break between lessons.

4 *I usually have / I'm usually having* lunch with a friend, but today *I have / I'm having* lunch with my brother.

2 **Complete the email with the present simple or present continuous form of the verbs in brackets.**

> ‹ Inbox   2 Messages   ⌃ ⌄
>
> Hi Daniela,
>
> How are you? ¹ _____ (I / have) a great time on holiday. At home, ² _____ usually _____ (I / not do) a lot of sports but here it's different. I'm here with my brother Noah, and ³ _____ (we / try) some new activities. Today we went canoeing. Now we're really tired and ⁴ _____ (Noah / sleep) on the sofa. But it was fun! I ⁵ _____ (not like) cold water but the water in the lake here is quite warm so we went swimming, too. ⁶ _____ (you / know) this area? It's really beautiful.
>
> What ⁷ _____ (you / do) at the moment? ⁸ _____ (you / study) for your exams? I know your father is a teacher . ⁹ _____ often _____ (he / help) you with your schoolwork? Anyway, ¹⁰ _____ (I / hope) you get good results in the exams.
>
> See you soon,
>
> Tina

ADJECTIVES: WORD ORDER

When we want to describe something, we can put adjectives and other classifiers before a noun. These words come in a specific order:

`opinion` `size` `age` `shape` `colour`
`origin (place)` `material`

a **big**, **round** hat (size, shape)
an **old American** car (age, origin)
a **lovely**, **red leather** bag (opinion, colour, material)

We do not usually use more than three adjectives before a noun.

3 **Complete the text with the words in brackets in the correct order.**

We're going camping next weekend. It's a bit cold so I'll need some ¹ _____ (clothes / warm / good). I saw a ² _____ (red / jumper / woollen) in a shop last week and I want it, but it's expensive! I'd like a new tent, too, but we don't really need it. We've got a(n) ³ _____ (round / ugly / tent) and dad says it's good enough. I've got a pair of ⁴ _____ (Italian / new / shoes) that I love but I'm not wearing them for camping. They'll get dirty!

UNIT 2

PAST SIMPLE

Regular verbs

The past simple of regular verbs is verb + -ed, e.g. *watched*, *looked*, etc. However, for verbs ending:

- consonant + -y: change -y to -ied, e.g. *tried*, *studied*, etc.
- vowel + consonant (with stress on the last syllable): double the final consonant and add -ed, e.g. *stopped*, *planned*, etc.
- vowel + -l: double the l and add -ed, e.g. *travelled*, *controlled*, etc.

Irregular verbs

- Irregular verbs have different forms in the past simple, e.g. *have → had*, *go → went*, etc.
  See page 128 for a list of irregular verbs.

We use the **past simple** to talk about:

- completed actions in the past, often with the time when they happened.
  *I **hung out** with friends yesterday.*
  *We **didn't go** to the cinema on Saturday afternoon.*
- two or more actions which happened after one another.
  *Meri **watched** a film and then she **went** to bed.*

PAST CONTINUOUS

We use the **past continuous** to talk about actions and events in progress at a particular time in the past.
At lunchtime, I was drawing cartoons for my blog.
We weren't playing computer games at 7 pm.
Was the teacher riding her new motorbike?

We can use the **past simple** to describe an action that interrupted an another action that was in progress in the **past continuous**.
*While we **were having** a barbecue, my cousins **arrived**.*
*My cousins **arrived** while we **were having** a barbecue.*

1 Choose the correct words to complete the sentences.

1 I was hanging out with friends when I *saw / was seeing* a film star.
2 I found a wallet on the floor but I *didn't know / wasn't knowing* what to do.
3 When the storm came, luckily we *didn't sail / weren't sailing* on the lake.

PAST PERFECT

We form the past perfect with *had* + the past participle. Sometimes *had* can be shortened to *'d*.
I had looked carefully. / I'd looked carefully.
I hadn't looked carefully.
Had you looked carefully?

- We use the past perfect to talk about events or actions which happened some time before another action or event in the past.
- The main past action is usually in the past simple.
  *When I **got** to the theatre, I realised **I'd left** my dance shoes at home.*

2 Complete the sentences with the past perfect form of the verbs in brackets.

1 When I got to Sara's party, I realised that I _____ (leave) her present at home.
2 My sister _____ (not get) back by the time I left home.
3 My friends didn't go to the cinema because they _____ (see) all the films.
4 I _____ (not be) a DJ before so I felt very nervous.

3 Choose the correct words to complete the story.

I ¹ *had / was having / 'd had* breakfast quietly on my own when my sister ² *came / was coming / 'd come* into the kitchen, shouting 'We're late!' As we ³ *got / were getting / 'd got* ready to leave, we ⁴ *heard / were hearing / 'd heard* a strange noise in the kitchen. Our dog ⁵ *found / was finding / had found* an empty milk carton and he ⁶ *played / was playing / 'd played* with it. We ⁷ *tidied up / were tidying up / 'd tidied up* the mess quickly. We ⁸ *ran / were running / 'd run* for the bus but we ⁹ *were / were being / 'd been* three minutes late. We ¹⁰ *missed / were missing / 'd missed* it! While I ¹¹ *thought / was thinking / 'd thought* about what to do next, my sister suddenly ¹² *said / was saying / 'd said*, 'Hang on, Jake, it's a holiday today! We don't have to go to school!'

PRESENT PERFECT

We form the present perfect of regular and irregular verbs with *has / have* + past participle.

We **haven't seen** the zebras.

Has she **taken** a photo of the sharks?

- In regular verbs the past participle looks the same as the past simple (verb + -*(e)d*).
  It **started**.   It **has started**.

- In irregular verbs the past participle sometimes looks the same as the past simple and sometimes it is different.
  We **found** her.   We **have found** her.
  I **saw** no one.   I**'ve seen** no one.

  We use the present perfect to talk about experiences in the past which have some link to the present.
  I've taken a photo of the sharks. (= Look at this photo.)

PAST SIMPLE

See Unit 2 page 115 for the past simple form and more information about its use.

PRESENT PERFECT AND PAST SIMPLE

We can use the **present perfect** to talk about experiences in our life up to the present.

- We don't use past time phrases with the **present perfect**.
  They've taken lots of photos.
  We haven't visited the wildlife park.

- We use *for* to introduce the length of time something lasted.
  for three months, for two years, for a long time

- We use *since* to introduce when something began.
  since four o'clock, since my birthday party

- When there is a verb after *since*, it is in the past simple.
  I have known him since I was eleven / since I started school / since I moved here.

- We can also use *just, already* and *yet* with the present perfect.
  just

- means 'only a short time ago' and it goes before the main verb in positive sentences.
  I've just seen a kangaroo over there.
  already

- means 'some time before now'. It emphasises that the action is now complete.

- goes before the main verb in positive sentences.
  I've already seen that film. Can we watch something else?

yet

- means 'up to now'. It often emphasises that we expected something to happen before now.

- goes at the end of a negative sentence.
  We haven't found the penguins yet. Shall we look for them?

- goes at the end of a question.
  Have you uploaded your photos yet?

1 Complete the conversations with the present perfect or past simple form of the verbs in brackets or a suitable word.

1. A: How long _____ you _____ (know) your best friend?
   B: I _____ (know) her since we _____ (start) primary school together.

2. A: _____ you ever _____ (sail) down a canal?
   B: Yes, I _____ .
   A: When _____ you _____ (do) that?
   B: I _____ (go) with my family last year.

3. A: _____ you _____ (see) that new science-fiction series yet?
   B: I _____ (already / see) that one but I _____ (not see) the comedy series yet. Everyone's talking about it!
   A: I _____ (just / finish) that. It's really funny!

USED TO

Positive / Negative forms

I, You, He, She, It, We, They	used to	live in a small village.
	didn't use to	

Question forms and short answers

Did	I, you, he, she, it, we, they **use to**	go for long walks?
Yes,	I, you, he, she, it, we, they	did.
No,		didn't.

- We use *used to* + verb to talk about habits or situations in the past which are not the same now.
  We used to walk to school. (= We don't walk to school now.)
  I didn't use to like going hiking. (= I enjoy it now.)

2 Rewrite the second sentence so that it means the same as the first sentence. Use the correct form of *used to*.

1. My family went camping very often in the past, but now we don't.

2. My dad had long hair when he was a teenager, but now it's short.

3. Did your friends play basketball when they were younger?

4. When we were at primary school, we didn't do much homework.

UNIT 4

MODAL VERBS

SHOULD

- *Should* has only one form.

| I, You, He, She, We, They | **should** tidy the living room. |
| | **shouldn't** make a mess. |

- We use *should* to give advice or make suggestions.
  I should buy a present for my mum.
  They should build a new sports centre.
- We use *shouldn't* when we think it isn't a good idea to do something.
  You shouldn't do your homework in front of the TV.
  We shouldn't eat too many chips.
- We use *should* in questions when we ask for advice.
  What should I say in my interview?
  Which shoes should I wear with this dress?

HAVE TO, HAVE GOT TO, MUST

- *Have to* and *have got to* change form.

I, You, We, They	**have to / have got to** go to school.
	don't have to go in the car.
He, She	**has to / has got to** be home by 10 pm.
	doesn't have to do any homework today.

- *Must/mustn't* have only one form.

| I, You, He, She, We, They | *must* catch the early bus. |
| | *mustn't* be late. |

- We use *must* and *have to / have got to* to talk about obligation.
  You must be 18 to see that film.
  He has to practise the guitar every day.
- We use *mustn't* when something isn't allowed.
  I mustn't sleep in class.
  You mustn't read that letter.

NEED TO AND NEEDN'T

- *Need to* changes form, and we usually use *needn't* as the negative form.

I, You, We, They	*need to* go to be earlier.
	needn't get up early. It's Saturday.
He, She	*needs to* get more sleep.
	needn't walk to school today.

- *Needn't* usually means the same as *don't / doesn't have to.*
  *I have some homework but I **needn't / don't have to** finish it today.*

- When we talk about things that are generally not necessary, we use *don't / doesn't have to.*
  My dad doesn't have to work on Sundays.

1 A school group is going to an adventure sports camp for a week. Read the notice and choose the correct verbs.

> **BLOGS** ⌄   **NEWSLETTERS** ⌄   **VIDEOS** ⌄
>
> There are eight different activities to choose from. You [1] *should / don't have to* look at the list of activities for the week and decide which ones you want to do. You can choose to do something different every day. You [2] *must / needn't* let us know if you want to be in the same group as your friends. You [3] *shouldn't / have got to* try at least three different activities in the week, but you [4] *don't have to / must* try everything. You [5] *mustn't / need to* sign up for activities before breakfast every day. You [6] *don't have to / mustn't* miss the safety lesson before each new activity, but you [7] *needn't / have got to* go to more than one safety lesson per sport. You [8] *shouldn't / have to* take part in an activity if you feel sick.

OBLIGATION IN THE PRESENT AND PAST

HAVE TO, HAD TO AND MUST

- The past form of *have to / have got to* is *had to.*
- There is no past tense of *must*. We use the past form *had to.*
  You had to be 18 to see that film.
  He had to practise the guitar every day.
- *Didn't have to* means that it was not necessary to do something.
  I didn't have to do a test.

2 Rewrite the sentences using the past form.

1 I must study hard for the exams next week.
  I _____ last week.

2 We have to take the bus to school today.
  _____ yesterday.

3 We must do extra training before our next football match.
  _____ our last football match.

BE GOING TO AND THE PRESENT CONTINUOUS FOR FUTURE ARRANGEMENTS

- We use the present continuous, usually with the time mentioned, for arrangements someone has made.
  I'm flying to Spain at the weekend.
  What time are you leaving?
- We use am / is / are (not) + going to + verb to make the *be going to* future.
- We use *be going to* for things we plan to do in the future.
  I'm going to visit Italy one day.
  Are you going to play?
- Sometimes both *be going to* and the present continuous are possible when you talk about the future.
- The present continuous is more likely when an appointment is mentioned.
  I'm seeing the doctor at 3 o'clock.

1 **Choose the correct form of the verbs to complete the sentences.**

1 Carrie wants to get fitter so *she's going to try / she's trying* some different sports to see which ones she enjoys.

2 I need to be at my sports club early tomorrow so *I'm taking / I'm going to take* the bus at half past seven.

3 Mum really enjoyed that cake we had at my cousin's party. *I'm going to ask / I'm asking* my aunt how to make it.

4 Chris *is going to take / is taking* his driving test on Monday morning, so *he's going to do / he's doing* lots of practice this weekend.

2 **Complete the conversation with the correct form of *be going to* and the words in brackets.**

A: [1] Are _____ (you, go) to my cousin Felix's party?

B: Yes, I think so.

A: What [2] _____ (wear)?

B: I'm not sure. My blue dress, probably.

A: My mum [3] _____ (bake) a birthday cake for him. Her cakes are delicious.

B: Great! [4] _____ (I, not make) any food, but I can take something to drink.

A: Good idea. [5] _____ (you, take) him a present?

B: I guess I should give him something.

A: [6] _____ (I, give) him this belt.

B: Oh, that's cool. [7] _____ (I, not have) much time to look for a good present.

A: We can give it as a shared present if you like.

B: Oh, that's great, thanks very much. But I [8] _____ (I, tell) him you found it for him.

PRESENT SIMPLE FOR THE FUTURE

We can use the present simple to talk about events that are fixed in timetables, or to say when a future event begins or ends. We sometimes call it the 'timetable future'.

*Our plane **arrives** at 10.30 tomorrow morning.*
*When **does** the concert **start**?*

3 **Complete the conversation with the verbs in the present simple and words from the timetable.**

arrive begin catch end leave meet

1 pm	meet at school gate
1.15 pm	bus to city centre
2 pm	play begins
3.45 pm	play ends
4.10 pm	bus back to school, arrives 4.30

Mum: So, you have a trip to the theatre tomorrow. Great! What time do you leave the school?

Dave: We [1] _____ at the school gate at one o'clock and then we go to the bus stop and [2] _____ to the city centre at a quarter past one.

Mum: What time [3] _____?

Dave: At two o'clock.

Mum: And what time [4] _____?

Dave: At a quarter to four. And then the bus back to school [5] _____ at ten past four. We [6] _____ at the school at four thirty.

CAN FOR ABILITY

We use *can/can't* to talk about ability or inability in the present. To talk about ability or inability in the past, we use *could/couldn't*. They are followed by the infinitive without *to*.

*I **can run** a kilometre without stopping.*

*She **could read** at four years old.*

- When we are talking about general ability **in the past**, we generally use *could* or *couldn't* + infinitive without *to*.

  *When I was five I **could run** quite fast, but I **couldn't swim**.*

- We use *will be able to* + infinitive to describe ability in the future.

  *In the future, we **will be able to travel** to other countries in seconds.*

1 Complete the sentences with the correct form of *can* and the verbs in brackets.

  1 When my mum was younger, she _____ (run) faster than everyone in her school.

  2 My brother's a drummer. He _____ (play) the drums really well, but he _____ (not sing).

  3 _____ we _____ (buy) food at the supermarket tomorrow? Don't forget, it's a holiday.

PRESENT AND PAST PASSIVE

We form the passive with the verb *be* + the past participle. Depending on whether we want to talk about the present or the past, we change the form of *be*.

Active	Passive
Present	
We **tidy** our classroom every day.	Our classroom **is tidied** every day.
I **don't clean** my shoes every day.	My shoes **aren't cleaned** every day.
Do they **call** you Nik or Nikky?	**Are** you **called** Nik or Nikky?
Past	
They **built** our school in 1995.	Our school **was built** in 1995.
They **didn't steal** your keys.	Your keys **weren't stolen**.
Did they **invite** you to the party?	**Were** you **invited** to the party?

We use the passive:

- when we are more interested in the person or thing affected by the action.

  We aren't allowed to eat in class.

- when we do not know who or what does the action.

  My cushions were made in Portugal.

- when it isn't important to say who or what does the action.

  Our exam results were published online.

  We include *by* when we want to emphasise who or what does the action.

  *The roof of our house was damaged **by the storm**.*

2 Rewrite the second sentence so that it means the same as the first. Use the present or past passive. Only include *by* if it is important.

  1 Thieves stole ten bicycles last week in town.
  Ten bicycles _____ last week in town.

  2 Someone designs a clever new app every day.
  A clever new app _____ every day.

  3 A film star owned that house before.
  That house _____ before.

  4 They didn't give me this bike for my birthday.
  I _____ for my birthday.

3 Complete the text with the correct active or passive form of the verbs in brackets. Use the past or present tense.

My friends and I [1] _____ (enjoy) hanging out together but there [2] _____ (be) nowhere to go when it rains. However, last week we [3] _____ (give) the keys to a beach hut. It [4] _____ (belong) to my family but it [5] _____ (not use) at all now. My uncle [6] _____ (have) some spare paint, but he didn't have time to help us so we [7] _____ (paint) the hut ourselves. It [8] _____ (finish) in two days. The table and chairs [9] _____ (find) next to the rubbish bin, we [10] _____ (make) the cushion covers and curtains and our families [11] _____ (give) us stuff for the kitchen area. Now we [12] _____ (need) to buy some food. It isn't huge but it's ours!

UNIT 7

FUTURE POSSIBILITY (*WILL*, *MAY* AND *MIGHT*)

We use *will*, *may* and *might* to talk about future possibilities.

- We use *will* with the infinitive when something is sure to happen in the future.
  You'll pass this exam with high marks! (= I'm sure.)
- We use *won't* with the infinitive if it is impossible.
  We won't go skiing. There isn't any snow. (= It's impossible.)
- We use *may* or *might* with the infinitive when something is possible but not certain.
  I may / might watch a film later. (= It's possible but I'm not sure.)
- We don't often use *may* or *might* to ask questions about future possibilities. We usually use *will*.
  Will you take something to eat? I may / might.

1 Complete the sentences with *will*, *may* or *won't*.

1 I'm sure I _____ go swimming after school. The sea looks perfect today.
2 We _____ have pizza or we _____ have a burger. We haven't decided yet.
3 My mum _____ be able to drive us to the concert, but she isn't sure.
4 Don't worry. I'm certain they _____ be late. They left 45 minutes ago.
5 Please come to the party. It _____ be a lot of fun, I'm sure.
6 My shoulder still hurts, so I _____ go to training after school. Can you tell the coach?

MODAL VERBS OF DEDUCTION (*MUST, MAY, MIGHT, COULD* AND *CAN'T*)

We use modal verbs of deduction *must*, *may*, *might*, *could* and *can't* to say what we can't see, but think is happening.

- To talk about something we think is certain, we use *must* + verb.
  You've done three tests, played a match and walked home. You must be tired. (= I'm certain you're tired)
- To talk about something we think is possible, we use *may*, *might* or *could* + verb.
  Mia isn't in class. She may/might/could be ill. (= Perhaps she's ill).

- To talk about something we think is not probable, we use *may* or *might* + *not* + verb. We don't use *could*.
  Petra's at the dentist. She may/might not come to training. (= Perhaps she won't come.)
- To talk about something we think is impossible, we use *can't* + verb (NOT *mustn't* + verb).
  We've just had maths. We can't have maths again this afternoon. (= I'm sure we don't have maths.)
- We don't use *can* to talk about deductions.

2 Choose the correct words to complete the conversation.

Becca: Who's this present from? There isn't a name on it.

Liz: Is it from your sister?

Becca: It ¹ *can't / must* be from her. I've already opened her present.

Liz: Is it from your grandparents?

Becca: It ² *could / must* be from them, I guess.

Liz: Well, the card ³ *might / can't* be inside.

Becca: Yes! The wrapping paper is really beautiful. It ⁴ *must / can't* be something special.

Liz: It's not very big. It ⁵ *may / must* be some jewellery. Did you ask for some?

Becca: No. Anyway, it's hard at one end and softer at the other, so it ⁶ *can't / might* be that. Oh, wow! It's some art brushes! And here's the card. It says 'Love from Liz'! Thank you!

Liz: Not at all!

3 Complete the second sentence so that it means the same as the first. Use *must, may, might, could* or *can't*.

1 My computer is very slow. I'm sure it's broken.
   My computer _____ broken.
2 I don't believe those shoes belong to you. They're much too big.
   Those shoes _____ to you.
3 I saw Mel in front of that old house on Green Street. I'm sure she lives there.
   Mel _____ in that old house on Green Street.
4 It's possible that my teacher speaks three languages. I'm not sure.
   My teacher _____ three languages.
5 Jon isn't wearing a sweater. Perhaps he doesn't feel cold.
   Jon _____ cold.
6 It's not possible that it's Mark at the door. He's away at the moment.
   It _____ Mark.

120 | GRAMMAR REFERENCE AND PRACTICE

FIRST CONDITIONAL

Conditional sentences tell us about a possible situation and a result. They use two clauses: the conditional clause and a result clause.

- The conditional clause begins with *if*.
- The conditional clause or the result clause can come first without changing the meaning.
- The first conditional uses the present simple in the conditional clause and the *will* future in the result clause.
- *If* + present tense, + *will/won't*
  *If we **go** to the cinema on foot, we'**ll save** money.*
  *If we **take** the bus, we **won't get** wet.*
- We use a comma when the *if* clause comes first.
- We can also put the *if* clause at the end of a sentence.
  We'll save money if we go there on foot.
- We use the first conditional to talk about possible or probable future events.
  If the sun shines, we'll go to the beach.
  We won't go to the beach if the sun doesn't shine.

1 Choose the correct form of the verbs to complete the sentences.

1 If *I don't go / I won't go* to bed soon, *I'm / I'll be* really tired tomorrow morning.
2 *I'll buy / I buy* some ice cream later if the café *is / will be* still open.
3 *You pass / You'll pass* your driving test if *you won't make / you don't make* any mistakes.
4 *We'll phone / We phone* my dad after the party if *we'll need / we need* a lift home.

ZERO CONDITIONAL

- The zero conditional uses the present simple in the conditional clause and in the result clause.
- *If* + present tense, + present tense
  *If plants **have** enough light, they **grow** well.*
- We use a comma when the *if* clause comes first.
- We can also put the *if* clause at the end of a sentence.
  *Plants **grow** well if they **have** enough light.*
- We use the zero conditional to talk about things that are true or always happen.
  If you give plants enough food and water, they grow well.
- *If* usually means the same as *when* in zero conditional sentences.
  *Plants grow well **when** you give them enough food and water.*

2 Complete the zero conditional sentences with the correct form of the verbs in brackets.

1 Everyone _____ sleepy if the weather _____ too hot. (feel, be)
2 If my brother _____ any money, he always _____ it on clothes. (earn, spend)
3 Students _____ stressed if their teacher _____ them too many tests. (get, give)
4 If I _____ a film, I _____ it to the end. (not like, not watch)

IF, WHEN AND UNLESS

- We use *if* for things that may happen.
  If you go to the beach, I'll see you there.
- We use *when* for things that will happen.
  When I arrive at the station my mum will pick me up.
- *Unless* means the same as *if not*.
  I'll stay at home unless it stops raining. (= If it doesn't stop raining.)

3 Complete the conversation with *if, when* or *unless*.

Lou: Are you going to Zoe's party tomorrow?
Ben: I don't know. I don't feel well today but I'll go to the party [1] _____ I feel better tomorrow.
Lou: Oh, I hope you feel better, then. I won't go [2] _____ you go, too.
Ben: But why not?
Lou: Because I'm too shy! I sometimes go to parties alone but [3] _____ I arrive, I always feel a bit nervous.
Ben: But you won't be alone. You know Zoe. She'll be disappointed [4] _____ you aren't there. OK, look, I'll go to the party. I won't stay at home [5] _____ I'm really sick. But I think I'll be OK.
Lou: Great! And will you message me [6] _____ you're ready to leave your house? Then we can go together.

4 Rewrite the sentences using *unless*.

1 I can't get up in the morning if I don't have enough sleep.
2 We'll all have dinner together if my mum doesn't get home too late.
3 My parents will go mad if we don't clear up this mess.
4 If we don't find a taxi soon, we'll miss the train.

UNIT 9

RELATIVE CLAUSES

DEFINING RELATIVE CLAUSES

- Defining relative clauses give essential information about the things, places or people we are talking about. They are never separated from the rest of the sentence by commas.

  *The cakes **that my brother makes** are really good.*

  We need the words *that my brother makes* to know which cakes the speaker is talking about.

- To begin a relative clause, we use the pronouns *who* (for people), *which* (for things), *that* (for things and people), *whose* (belonging to) and *where* (for places).

  *There's the girl **who** won the cookery competition.*

  *She showed me the recipe **which** she invented.*

  *That's the boy **whose** mum designs sunglasses.*

  *This is the place **where** I bought my book.*

- *Who, which* or *that* can be the **subject** or the **object** of the relative clause.

  *The woman **who/that** runs the café is very friendly.* (*who/that* is the **subject**)

  *There's the chef **who/that** I told you about.* (*who/that* is the **object**)

- We can leave out *who, which* or *that* if it is the object of the defining clause.

  There's the chef I told you about.

1 **Complete the sentences with *who, which, where* or *whose*.**

1 The first restaurant _____ my dad worked was in London.

2 The job _____ he did was not very well paid.

3 I've never met anyone _____ could cook as well as my mum.

4 The person _____ job I would like most is a chef with a TV show.

2 **Look at the sentences in Exercise 1 and answer the questions.**

1 Where can you use *that* instead of the word you chose?

2 Where can you leave out the relative pronoun?

NON-DEFINING RELATIVE CLAUSES

- We use non-defining relative clauses to give more information about the things or people we are talking about. Non-defining relative clauses are always separated from the rest of the sentence by commas.

  *The cakes on this plate**, which my brother helped to make,** are really good.*

  If we take out *which my brother helped to make*, we still know which cakes the speaker is talking about.

- Non-defining relative clauses begin with the relative pronoun *who* (for people), *where* (for places), *which* (for things) or *whose*, but <u>never</u> that.

  My brother, who is an excellent cook, has written a cookbook.

  The recipes, which he tested carefully, require lots of special ingredients.

  NOT *The recipes, that he tested carefully, …*

- We can never leave out the relative pronoun in a non-defining clause.

3 **Combine the pairs of sentences into one sentence. Use non-defining relative clauses.**

1 My grandma taught me to make cakes. She works in a bakery.

2 Small bakeries often produce the best bread. They can be hard to find.

3 I admire farmers. They do an essential and hard job.

4 **Explain the difference in meaning between the pairs of sentences.**

1 a The biscuits which my brother made were all eaten.

  b The biscuits, which my brother made, were all eaten.

2 a The students who had not had lunch wanted to find a café.

  b The students, who had not had lunch, wanted to find a café.

COMPARISONS WITH (*NOT*) AS … AS

When we compare two things:

- we can use *as + adjective + as* to say the things are the same.

  *In my school, pizza is **as popular as** burgers.*

- we can use *not as + adjective + as* to say two things are different.

  *Chocolate cake isn**'t as healthy as** fruit salad.*

- The form of the adjective doesn't change with *as + adjective + as*.

  *A burger isn**'t as big as** a pizza.* (NOT *as bigger as …*)

5 **Complete the sentences with (*not*) as … as.**

1 I'm short, but my sister is very short.

  I'm not ___as short as my sister___ .

2 The burger bar is popular. The pizza restaurant is popular, too.

  The burger bar is _____.

3 Ireland is wet. Scotland is wet, too.

  Ireland is _____.

4 Lemonade is sweet, but cola is really sweet.

  Lemonade is _____.

UNIT 10

SECOND CONDITIONAL

We use the second conditional to talk about an unlikely or impossible situation in the present or future, and its results.

Possible situation (*if* clause)	Result (main clause)
If I had more time,	I'd (would) set up my own video channel.

- We sometimes use *I were* instead of *I was* in the conditional clause.
  *If **I were** a journalist, I'd (would) meet lots of famous people.*
- When we **give advice**, we often say, *If I was (or were) you, I'd …*
  If I were you, I'd consider doing a course in video making.
- We often use the second conditional to ask questions.
  If you had the chance, would you visit California?
- We answer the questions with the conditional tense.
  I wouldn't visit California, I'd go to Hawaii.

1 **Complete the sentences with the correct second conditional form of the verbs in brackets.**

1 If I _____ (win) an important prize, I _____ (be) really happy.
2 My brother _____ (buy) a better laptop if he _____ (have) enough money.
3 If my cousins _____ (not live) so far way, I _____ (hang out) with them more often.
4 If I _____ (be) you, I _____ (go) to bed much earlier.
5 What _____ you _____ (do) if you _____ (see) a celebrity?

2 **Answer the questions with complete sentences.**

1 What would you do if you lost your phone?
  If I lost my phone, _____.
2 If you could live anywhere in the world, where would you live?
  If I could live anywhere in the world, _____.
3 What would you do if you saw a classmate cheating in an exam?
4 I don't want to go to my best friend's party. What should I do?

THIRD CONDITIONAL

Possible situation (*if* clause)	Result (main clause)
If I'd (had) lived in the 18th century,	I'd (would) have played the violin with Mozart.

- We use the third conditional to talk about an unreal situation in the past and its results.
  If I had known it was your birthday, I would have bought you a present. (= I didn't know it was your birthday, so I couldn't have bought you a present.)

3 **Choose the correct words to complete the third conditional sentences.**

1 She *had caught / would have caught* the bus if she *had woken up / would have woken up* earlier.
2 If I *hadn't lost / wouldn't have lost* my phone, I *had phoned / would have phoned* you.
3 My friends *hadn't known / wouldn't have known* about the concert if I *hadn't told / wouldn't have told* them.
4 If you *had arrived / would have arrived* five minutes earlier, you *could have / could have had* some cake.

4 **Rewrite the second sentence so that it means the same as the first. Use the third conditional.**

1 The bus was late so they missed the film.
  If the bus hadn't been late, _____.
2 She wanted to take photos of the view but she didn't have a camera.
  If she had had her camera, _____.
3 We didn't win the match because we played badly.
  If we hadn't _____.
4 My friends didn't go skateboarding because it was raining.
  My friends would _____.

UNIT 1 SPEAKING

PAGE 12, EXERCISE 3

Student A

You have one minute to describe your photo to your partner. Remember to use adjectives and to use phrases to give yourself thinking time if you need it.

UNIT 4 VOCABULARY

PAGE 38, EXERCISE 4

1 False. It's football, with knee and ankle injuries the most common.
2 False. Your skin is thickest on the bottom of your feet (including *under* your heel) and the inside of your hands. It's thinnest at your eyes.
3 All true.
4 False. Breathing in deeply can make your heart beat faster and make you feel more stressed! Breathing *out* slowly helps you feel calm, and you may recover *a little* faster if you are not too stressed.

UNIT 4 SPEAKING

UNIT 1 SPEAKING

PAGE 12, EXERCISE 5

Student B

You have one minute to describe your photo to your partner. Student A, give your partner feedback using the checklist on page 12, Exercise 4.

PAGE 85, EXERCISE 8

You and three friends were out sailing on a large boat when a storm started. It took you a long way from land, and now your boat is sinking! Luckily, there is a small lifeboat with space for four people and a few items. Decide which five items you will take to survive until you are rescued.

- ✔ a large bottle of water
- ✔ a packet of biscuits
- ✔ a fishing rod
- ✔ a map of the sea you are in
- ✔ four red rain coats
- ✔ a mirror
- ✔ a long rope
- ✔ one life vest

IRREGULAR VERBS

Infinitive	Past simple	Past participle	Translation	Infinitive	Past simple	Past participle	Translation
be	was/were	been		learn	learned/learnt	learned/learnt	
beat	beat	beaten		lend	lent	lent	
become	became	become		let	let	let	
begin	began	begun		lie	lied	lied	
bite	bit	bitten		light	lit	lit	
bleed	bled	bled		lose	lost	lost	
blow	blew	blown		make	made	made	
break	broke	broken		mean	meant	meant	
bring	brought	brought		meet	met	met	
build	built	built		pay	paid	paid	
burn	burned/burnt	burned/burnt		put	put	put	
buy	bought	bought		read	read	read	
catch	caught	caught		ride	rode	ridden	
choose	chose	chosen		ring	rang	rung	
come	came	come		rise	rose	risen	
cost	cost	cost		run	ran	run	
cut	cut	cut		say	said	said	
dig	dug	dug		see	saw	seen	
do	did	done		sell	sold	sold	
draw	drew	drawn		send	sent	sent	
dream	dreamed/dreamt	dreamed/dreamt		shine	shone	shone	
drink	drank	drunk		shoot	shot	shot	
drive	drove	driven		show	showed	shown	
eat	ate	eaten		shut	shut	shut	
fall	fell	fallen		sing	sang	sung	
feel	felt	felt		sit	sat	sat	
fight	fought	fought		sleep	slept	slept	
find	found	found		speak	spoke	spoken	
fly	flew	flown		spell	spelled/spelt	spelled/spelt	
forget	forgot	forgotten		spend	spent	spent	
get	got	got		stand	stood	stood	
give	gave	given		steal	stole	stolen	
go	went	gone		swim	swam	swum	
grow	grew	grown		take	took	taken	
hang	hung	hung		teach	taught	taught	
have	had	had		tear	tore	torn	
hear	heard	heard		tell	told	told	
hide	hid	hidden		think	thought	thought	
hit	hit	hit		throw	threw	thrown	
hold	held	held		understand	understood	understood	
hurt	hurt	hurt		wake	woke	woken	
keep	kept	kept		wear	wore	worn	
know	knew	known		win	won	won	
lead	led	led		write	wrote	written	
leave	left	left					